Why Fight?

The Causes of the American Civil War

Why Fight?

The Causes of the American Civil War

The House Divided
The Civil War

Corinne J. Naden & Rose Blue

RSVP
RAINTREE
STECK-VAUGHN
PUBLISHERS
A Steck-Vaughn Company

Austin, Texas

www.steck-vaughn.com

For Maire Plunkett Baldwin, my favorite college kid, with love, from Corinne
For my very good friend Sam Roth, with love, from Rose

Published by Raintree Steck-Vaughn Publishers,
an imprint of Steck-Vaughn Company

Publishing Director: Walter Kossmann
Editor: Shirley Shalit
Project Management & Design: Gino Coverty
Cover Design: Gino Coverty
Media Researcher: Margie Foster & Claudette Landry
Electronic Production: Scott Melcer & Gino Coverty

Consultant: Paul Finkelman, University of Tulsa, College of Law

Library of Congress Cataloging-in-Publication Data

Naden, Corinne J.
    Why Fight?: the causes of the American Civil War / Corinne J. Naden & Rose Blue.
        p.   cm. — (The house divided: the civil war)
    Includes index.
    Summary: Discusses the events leading up to the American Civil War, particularly the strongly held beliefs about the institution of slavery.
    ISBN 0-8172-5580-X
    1. United States — History — Civil War, 1861-1865 — Causes Juvenile literature.   [1. United States — History — Civil War, 1861-1865 — Causes. 2. Slavery — History.]   I. Blue, Rose.   II. Title.   III. Series: Naden, Corinne J. House divided.
    E459.N39   1999
    973.7'11 — dc21   99-20910
                                                                       CIP   AC

Printed and bound in the United States of America
1 2 3 4 5 6 7 8 9 0 IP 03 02 01 00 99

Cover photo: The famous debates between Abraham Lincoln and Stephen Douglas during the Senate race in 1858 took place throughout Illinois.

Title page photo: The Underground Railroad provided way stations from the South to Canada.

Acknowledgments listed on page 112 constitute part of this copyright page.

Contents

A Long Time Coming ... and Going

Prologue

Mary Chesnut of Charleston, South Carolina, was one of the first to hear it. "I sprang out of bed," she said, "and got on my knees to pray as I never prayed before." What Mary heard was the heavy booming of cannon. It was the start of the American Civil War, the most terrible fight in the nation's history.

Major Robert Anderson of Kentucky heard it, too. It was 4:30 in the morning, April 12, 1861. Anderson and his 68 U.S. soldiers were huddled behind the walls of Fort Sumter, the Federal outpost in Charleston Harbor. They'd been there since Christmas of 1860, cut off by the 6,000 militiamen of South Carolina just across the water. Last evening, Anderson had been told to surrender. This career U.S. army officer, who was sympathic to slavery, refused.

So, at 4:30 a.m., the war began. The order came from Pierre Gustave Toutant Beauregard of Louisiana. The Confederate general had a fine bushy mustache and a rather dapper air. He was quite impressed with his importance on this early morning. Of course, his critics felt that he was always impressed with his importance. When his glossy dark hair began to turn white in 1861, his friends said it was due to the burden of his duties. Others said it was due more to the fact that the Northern sea blockade had cut off the South's supply of hair dye. But perhaps Beauregard's importance this morning was because he felt a little

like a student getting back at a teacher. Major Anderson had once been his gun instructor.

For a day and a half, more than 3,000 shells rained down on the little island in Charleston Harbor. No soldiers died in the bombardment, although one horse did. In the end, of course, Anderson and his men had no choice. The U.S. troops surrendered. It was a splendid sight, this attack on Fort Sumter. At least it seemed that way to the citizens of Charleston. They ran to their rooftops to cheer each gun firing. They were fair, however, and cheered the Federal troops, too, for bravery under such a shelling. Mary Chesnut, passionately Southern but lukewarm about war, nevertheless found it so exciting that she could take no more than tea all day.

Charleston citizens watched and wept over the bombardment of Fort Sumter (center) from Cummings Point (right) and Fort Moultrie (left).

And so, in an atmosphere that resembled the opening of a county fair, began the costliest, deadliest, bloodiest, and most horrible war in U.S. history. Of all the U.S. and Confederate troops who fought in it, as many as 40 percent died or were wounded. More than 600,000 Americans lost their lives from all causes. All this bloodshed happened many years ago, between 1861 and 1865.

The American Civil War was like a family fight gone completely out of control. Only this time it was not just a family divided but a country divided, not just a divided house of three or five or even ten people, but a divided house of millions. This time the fight involved everybody. Virginians fought New Yorkers. So-called Yankees from Indiana aimed at so-called Johnny Rebs in Georgia. Sometimes people who lived on one street fought people who lived on the next. Worse yet, sometimes brother fought brother and father fought son.

THE WAR: WHAT DO WE CALL IT?

The American Civil War is sometimes called the U.S. Civil War, the War for the Union, the War for Southern Independence. Official reports of the U.S. Government refer to it as the War of the Rebellion. That is because the government regarded the secession of the southern states as a "rebellion" against the United States. An old-fashioned, and inaccurate, term for this conflict is the War Between the States. It was not. It was a war between the United States of America and the 11 states that seceded to form the Confederate States of America.

The Opposing Sides: What Do We Call Them? When speaking of the Northern troops, we may refer to them here as the United States, U.S., the Federals, the Blue (for the color of their uniforms), the Union, and occasionally by the nickname "Yankees." Southern troops may be the Confederates, the Gray (for the color of their uniforms), and sometimes by their nicknames "Rebels" or even "Johnny Reb."

Confederate leader and hero General Robert E. Lee knew how ghastly this conflict would be. As the storm clouds gathered, he told his sister, "We are in a state of war which will yield to nothing." Later on, he would lament, "It is well that war is so terrible for we would become too fond of it."

It was terrible indeed. More Americans fell in just two days, at the Battle of Shiloh on the Tennessee River, than in all previous U.S. wars! For three bloody days at Gettysburg, a Confederate army of about 75,000 fought courageously against a Federal force of some 90,000 men. The result was a defeat for the South, and the cost was enormous. A young farmer, Private Andrew Park of Mississippi, described it vividly. He said, "I could have walked a half or three quarters of a mile on the dead soldiers of the enemy and not have put my feet on the ground."

The Civil War was a long time coming, and its effects have been a long time going. Why is it so important to remember? Because it helps us to understand the kind of Americans we are today. Because in some ways, the Civil War is still with us. In some ways, we still see things in black and white. In some ways, the old wounds between North and South are still open. Virginians don't shoot at New Yorkers anymore, and they probably never will, but some of the old scars remain.

THE HIGH COST OF U.S. WARS

The total casualty list in any war includes those who died from sickness or accidents not involving battle or who are missing. These figures list battlefield deaths only.

War	Deaths
American Revolution (1775-83)	4,435
War of 1812 (1812-15)	2,260
Mexican War (1846-48)	1,733
Civil War (1861-65)	212,678
(North:138,154; South: 74,524)	
Spanish-Am. War (1898)	385
World War I (1917-18)	53,513
World War II (1941-46*)	292,131
Korean War (1950-53)	33,667
Vietnam War (1964-73)	47,369
Persian Gulf War (1991)	148

*Japan surrendered in August 1945, but war did not end until Presidential Proclamation on Dec. 31, 1946.
(Source: *The World Almanac*, 1998)

WAR TOUCHES EVERYONE

Twenty-one-year-old Austin Whipple of Concord, New Hampshire, was leading a quiet life with his family until patriotism stirred him to join the army. He wrote home, "Oh, brother, when we are away in New England, our imagination of horrors of these scenes are nothing but dreams."

Mary Ann Livermore, a young lady of Boston, wrote, "Women who had never before concerned themselves with politics took the daily papers to their rooms and wept over them."

With photos such as this, taken after the battle of Antietam (1862) by famed photographer Matthew Brady, war quickly loses any possible glamorous appeal.

How could this have happened? How could this strong, healthy country become so divided a house? Why did we turn against each other so violently? What would make brother shoot at brother, or neighbor try to kill a friend? Could anything be that important? Lots of people in the North and in the South said yes.

Family fights may happen in a flash, but civil wars don't. This one took a long time to get started. First, there were heated but polite arguments and then differences that grew nastier and were never settled. Ever so slowly, the people in the North and those in the South were pushed to opposite sides of a house in the process of dividing.

But why fight at all? Why couldn't differences be reasoned away? Because no matter how many times an argument was settled, one difference was never solved and would never go away. It was called slavery. It divided the North and the South like nothing else. And it all began years before the first shot, on April 12, 1861, that turned into the cruel, bloody, and terrible American Civil War.

Slavery:
We Agree to Disagree

How did our house get so divided? How did the United States get into such a mess? There we were back in 1860, the year before the Civil War, 33 states and more than 31 million people, tied together by one central government. We had a lot in common. Most Americans spoke the same language. Most professed a staunch belief in God and country. In fact, during his second inaugural speech in March 1865, with the war nearly over, Abraham Lincoln expressed these thoughts by saying, "Both [sides] read the same Bible and pray to the same God...." Most Americans thought that hard work would bring success. Most were proud of this tough young nation springing out of the wilderness.

There were differences, of course. There always had been. Besides the obvious differences in background and religion, right from the start people disagreed about how the country should be run and where it was going. And certainly no one was shy about criticizing America's leaders. Even the respected and admired George Washington faced some criticism during his administrations. Everyone was fair game. Alexander Hamilton didn't mind calling President John Adams unfit for public office, and Adams felt much the same way about Thomas Jefferson. James

The seeds that erupted into civil war began here, at slave auctions such as this 17th century one.

Buchanan got the worst of it, however. When he left the White House just before the Civil War, his critics said he was "the lowest in the dirty catalog of treasonable mischief-makers."

But all this shouting never turned to shooting. The conversation might have been spirited, indeed, but that was mostly all it was—just talk. In time, leaders and citizens alike solved their differences, more or less, and got on with building the country. So, what happened by the year 1861 to stop the talking and start the fighting? What turned stinging words into killing bullets? Why fight?

The answer was simple and terrible. Slavery. Nothing so divided the American house as did that one word—and all it stood for. At the bottom of every argument over states' rights or state borders or tariffs or personal freedom was that one single issue. It was there when the United States was born, and it was never, never settled until Americans began killing Americans in horrifying numbers.

A DIFFERENCE OF OPINION

"Just let them blue bellies set one foot on Georgia land," declared Lally Ross of the Third Augusta Volunteers. Private Ross was 16 years old and could not write his name. He had never owned a slave and would probably never be rich enough to own one, but he was willing to give up his life for slavery.

"It's not right to treat people that way. I don't care what color they are." That came from Richard Drayler, a 20-year-old lieutenant, 31st New York Cavalry. Drayler had a high school diploma and a strong conviction that slavery was wrong and the Union must be saved. This did not necessarily mean, however, that those who felt as Drayler did wanted to serve in battle next to a black man or live on the same street.

Emotions ran high on the slavery issue, even if people did not always understand what it was really about. How did slavery get here, and when? Even before the first Pilgrim landed at Plymouth, indentured servitude had appeared in the colonies. Back in 1619, a Dutch ship sailed into the harbor at Jamestown, Virginia. When it pulled up anchor, it left behind 20 black people from Africa.

They were sold to the English colonists as indentured servants, meaning they would work for a specified number of years and then supposedly be granted their freedom. These people had

EARLY SLAVE SOCIETIES

One of the first European societies to use slaves was Athens, in Ancient Greece. Until about 594 B.C., the wealthy of Athens kept fellow citizens as slaves, usually because the enslaved person owed money. When that kind of slavery was abolished, the rich had to look elsewhere. Wars with Persia and other lands brought in slave labor. By about the fourth century B.C., about one-third of the Athens population was slaves. That society was finally destroyed by Philip II of Macedonia in 338 B.C. At that time, most of the Athen slaves—but not all—were freed.

Rome was a slave society from about the second century B.C. to the fourth century A.D. Once again, successful wars created a great flood of captives. Eventually, about 30 percent of the Roman civilization was enslaved.

The famous and admired gladiators of Roman days were usually combat-trained slaves, perhaps captured in battle.

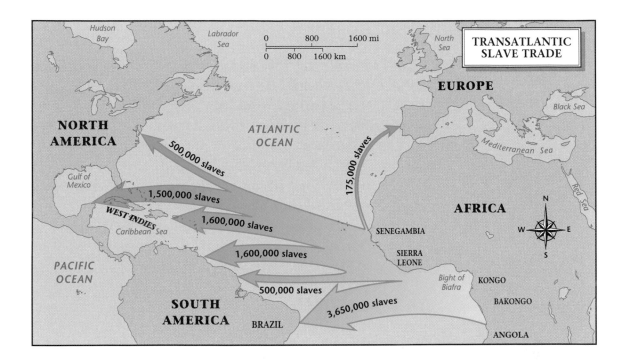

TRANSATLANTIC SLAVE TRADE

500,000 slaves

1,500,000 slaves

1,600,000 slaves

1,600,000 slaves

500,000 slaves

3,650,000 slaves

175,000 slaves

probably been slaves in the West Indies or Brazil, but they were not legally enslaved when they arrived in Virginia. However, by the end of the 17th century, black peoples' status as indentured laborers had deteriorated into that of slaves.

Slavery was not unique to the colonies, of course. By the time black slavery reached the Americas, slavery was a very old and time-honored institution. It has existed in various forms throughout all of recorded history. Ancient Egypt had slaves, as did most African societies. Slavery was accepted throughout Greek and Roman civilizations. Before Europeans arrived in America, some native peoples also kept slaves. When the Spanish conquered much of South America in the 16th century, they put the native Indian tribes to work in the mines and the fields. Unaccustomed to such harsh working conditions and exposed to diseases that were foreign to them, the Indians died in great numbers. So, the Spanish began importing slaves from Africa in

Millions of Africans were forced into the transatlantic slave trade between the early 16th and the 19th centuries. Thousands made the miserable sea voyage to North America, where they became a vital cog in the plantation economy of the South. Others were sent to the Caribbean islands and South America and Europe.

the early 1500s. Thus began the harsh practice of using slaves to work the plantation fields. When the American colonies and later the states began to develop profitable plantations, they, too, began importing slaves from Africa. A slave trade network was set up involving North America, the West Indies, and Africa.

By 1681, Virginia alone had about 2,000 slaves. Eventually, slavery was legal in all of the 13 original colonies. When the Constitutional Convention met in 1787 to form a new nation, five northern states had either banned slavery or taken steps to end it.

Since the main business of the convention was to set up a new government, the 55 delegates, many of whom were slaveholders, were not eager to talk about slavery. However, the delegates were quite aware that slavery was a touchy issue causing sectional disagreement in the new nation and that it needed to be discussed. So several compromiseses were reached. Among them, to satisfy the interests of southern planters, was the decision to extend consitutional protection to the African slave trade for 20 years. To soothe northern antislavery feelings, that protection could be annulled by law at the end of that period. It was also agreed that three-fifths of the slaves in a state would be counted when apportioning representation in Congress. However, they would be counted as property for purposes of taxation

Given these apparently satisfactory compromises of the Constitutional Convention, why did slavery become an issue so dividing that we went to war with each other? Because, as the country grew, slavery came to mean two very different things to the North and to the South. Certain groups, the Quakers for instance, opposed slavery on religious grounds; it was wrong. Some said it took jobs away from white workers. But no matter how anyone felt, slavery was illegal in the northern states. The North had become the country's industrial region. By the mid-19th century, the port cities of Boston, New York, and

Philadelphia were bustling with activity. Immigrants, mostly from Europe, were flocking to America's shores in search of a new life—and work. Merchants and shipbuilders and shopowners didn't need slaves. Lots of people would work for very little money. This, of course, made it easier for the North to be antislavery.

But the South was different. The South needed slavery, or so it thought. Here was a land of mild climate, fertile soil, and long growing seasons. There weren't many towns or villages and even fewer cities. Life was slower and less hectic than in the North. The South may not have had much industry, but it did have cotton. And "cotton is king!" cried Senator James Hammond of South Carolina. In fact, by midcentury, it accounted for more than half of all American exports.

Slavery was more than just a "peculiar domestic institution," as some Southern leaders called it. In the South, slavery was part of the culture, a sign of wealth and prestige. If you owned slaves, you were better off than someone who didn't. If you didn't own slaves, you hoped that someday you could.

Even more than part of the culture, the South thought slavery was necessary. Slaves made the plantations of the South work. That made the Southern economy work. And that meant money and prosperity. To grow these huge amounts of crops—tobacco, sugar, rice, cotton—the South needed the plantation system. Since farming was done largely by hand, it took a lot of people

WHAT PRICE FREEDOM?

"Manumission" means freeing from slavery. Outside of forbidding slavery altogether, or abolishing it as in the Thirteenth Amendment to the U.S. Constitution, how did slaves gain freedom? In some Islamic societies, a slave had to be freed after a certain number of years. In some African slave societies, children of a slave were born free. Sometimes a slave, if he or she could obtain the money, could simply buy freedom. Manumission was illegal in some Southern states and legal at various times in others. About 30,000 slaves were manumitted in Virginia from 1782 to 1806. By 1860, there were about 260,000 free blacks living in the South.

working in the fields to make cotton king and keep it on the throne. But plantations couldn't make money unless all that labor was cheap. What was cheaper than not paying anyone at all? Actually, slavery, not cotton, became king.

By 1860, just before the start of the Civil War, there were about four million slaves—men, women, and children—in the United States. Out of a U.S. population of some 31 million, that meant that one out of every seven Americans was owned by someone. That, indeed, is an amazing figure.

The U.S. Congress had years before stopped the international slave trade, although an illegal slave trade was operating. Of course, by this time, the slaves themselves were having children. At the start of the Civil War, most American slaves were American born.

Even though most slaves lived in the South, not every Southerner owned slaves. Far from it. In fact, the poorest white Southerners weren't much better off than many slaves in terms of food, shelter, and education. It was only the owners of huge plantations who could afford a large number of slaves. Most owners had no more than four. Many slaves were protected and well treated, if only because they were valuable property. Many others, perhaps most, were brutally treated—whipped, abused, degraded, and torn from their families. And that, perhaps, was the worst injustice of all—the breakup of the slave family.

Marriages, if allowed in the first place, were little more than a hoax. After all, the plantation owner was not interested in romance. What he was interested in was more slaves. A marriage ceremony might be performed, but it meant nothing in the eyes of the law. And if children followed the marriage, father, mother, and child sooner or later might be sold separately. The pain of that tearing apart, the damage done by the total disintegration of that family unit is still felt in African-American families today.

What was it like to be a slave in the American South? Whether captured in a foreign land or born in America, a slave would probably at one time or another face the auction block. Usually, the auction was in heavy operation between October and May. This allowed the newly purchased slave to become accustomed to his or her new surroundings before the next growing season.

The auction block was surely one of the most frightening and degrading of all human experiences. Made to stand in front of a group of white shoppers, the freshly scrubbed slaves were paraded like so much cattle. They were sometimes told to jump or dance to show good health, or made to undress so that a potential owner could see whether they had been whipped. The new owner wasn't particularly squeamish about whippings, but scar marks might mean that a slave was a troublemaker and, in the eyes of the owner, had to be disciplined. Rarely would a buyer assume that a slave owner was at fault for abusing a slave. The assumption was that the slave was at fault and had to be beaten.

On the very large plantations, slaves were often put to work in the fields beginning at age 12. From the first light of dawn until well into the dark, they toiled in the fields, with perhaps a few minutes of rest at noontime.

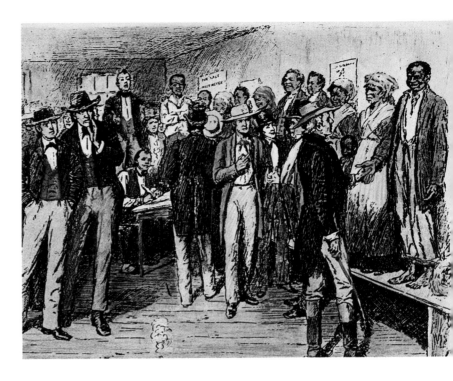

A future president of the United States, 19-year-old Abraham Lincoln (second from left) sees a slave auction for the first time.

And at the end of the long day, what did they have to look forward to? There were exceptions, of course, but most slaves were fed a poor diet. They might exist on "hog and hominy," which was corn and some fatty salted meat. They had poor quality, worn-out clothing, and the children were generally without shoes. Their medical care was practically nonexistent, although general medicine at the time was more likely to kill than heal anyway. Since slaves were valuable property, most owners took care of them.

How was it possible for a plantation owner, with only a few white men to help him, keep control over perhaps hundreds of slaves on the plantation? Why didn't the slaves just, by force of numbers, take over? The answer was simple—fear. It was the one thing slaves could count on every day of their lives, and it was a powerful deterrent. A wrong move, a wrong look could bring severe punishment, or even the auction block. The most common punishment was a beating, usually carried out in front of the other slaves.

Living with fear led to a sort of caste system among the slaves themselves for their own protection. The more valuable you were to the household, the less likely you would be sold or mistreated. At the bottom of the slave scale were the field hands. They could easily be replaced. But those who learned a skill such as carpentry or cooking, or who served the master or mistress in the "big house" became very valuable, even to the point of "lording" it over the other slaves in the household. This was survival at its very most basic.

How could they possibly have survived? Many didn't, of course. Others hung on to their sanity with dreams of freedom. In their few hours of free time—slaves were given time off on Sundays on most plantations—they tended to their own needs, or planted their own gardens, or told stories to their children.

When permitted, they might engage in riotous celebrations where they could dance and sing and dream of a better life that, for most, never came.

And suppose a slave did get up the courage to run away? Just where was he or she to go? The law, of course, would not help, and very few Southerners, whether slave owners or not, had the inclination, or the courage, to aid the runaway. And remember that the slave had no money, little clothing, no food, and was almost completely ignorant of the world outside the plantation. Most slaves could not read or write and, in fact, knew how to do little more than pick cotton or some other crop.

Yet, some slaves did escape to freedom, to the North, or even better, to the "promised land" of Canada. There were many ways of finding freedom. One of the most unusual involved Henry "Box" Brown. A white friend actually packed him in a crate and shipped him to the Antislavery Society headquarters in Philadelphia! He arrived in good shape—and free! Slaves did not generally escape via a shipping crate, but most did so on their own or with the help of friends. Others were aided by abolitionists and the famed Underground Railroad.

An abolitionist was someone who considered slavery to be a great sin against human rights. The hard core abolitionists usually based such feelings on religion and the Bible. Others felt that slavery was an economic and social evil. Still others, Abraham Lincoln among them, believed that although slavery was wrong, the government did not have the power to wipe it out where it already existed. Lincoln, however, believed that if slavery were not allowed to expand, the South would eventually end it.

In time, militant abolitionists would turn most Northerners against slavery. The movement that started it all had begun years before in a Baltimore, Maryland, jail. A 24-year-old editor from Massachusetts, William Lloyd Garrison, was arrested for denouncing in his newspaper a merchant who was legally ferrying slaves up and down the Atlantic coast.

While in jail, Garrison decided that slavery had to end—now. In January 1831, back in Boston, he begin publishing the newspaper called *The Liberator*. So, began the crusade in earnest. Two years later, Garrison and others founded the American Anti-Slavery Society. For the first time in America, men and women, both black and white, played a role in the organization.

Although most runaway slaves were captured within a day or two of escape, many did reach the North with the help of the Underground Railroad. This was neither underground nor a railroad. Instead, it was a loose network of safe places, called "stations," where escaped slaves, known as "packages" or "freight," were hidden and transported in darkness to the next stop on the way north. Those who aided the slaves were called "conductors" on the railroad, and many of them were former slaves, such as Harriet Tubman or Frederick Douglass. When Harriet Beecher Stowe, daughter of a New England preacher, wrote her famous novel of slavery, *Uncle Tom's Cabin*, she gained much knowledge from her contact with the Underground Railroad in Cincinnati, Ohio.

THE RADICAL GENIUS

Relentless and arrogant, William Lloyd Garrison was the radical genius of the abolitionist movement. Born in 1805 in Newburyport, Massachusetts, he spent his life preaching against slavery and inequality. A printer and newspaper editor, he lived by these words he printed in 1830: "He who opposes public liberty overthrows his own."

THE BOOK THAT STARTED A WAR

Uncle Tom's Cabin, or *Life Among the Lowly* (1852), by Harriet Beecher Stowe, inflamed both sides of the slavery issue by portraying slaves as human beings with dignity and feelings. It is the story, set in Kentucky and Louisiana, of Uncle Tom, a black slave who is well treated by his first two owners, George Shelby and Augustine St. Clare. Uncle Tom is devoted to Little Eva, St. Clare's daughter, who later dies in a touching scene. Uncle Tom also dies after he is savagely beaten by his third owner, Simon Legree, a Northerner by birth. The rest of the book concerns the flight of Eliza, a biracial woman, as she flees with her baby over the ice floes of the Ohio River. Later, she is joined by her husband George, who uses the Underground Railroad. The book was especially interesting in that it lent sympathy to the cause of the antislavery movment, and yet the villain of the story, Simon Legree, is from the North; the kind St. Clare is a Southerner.

Uncle Tom's Cabin turned the hearts and minds of thousands of Americans against the institution of slavery. Stowe succeeded so well that 300,000 copies of the novel were sold in a single year. Supposedly, some years after its publication, Abraham Lincoln met the author and said, "So you're the little lady that started this great war."

(top photo)
Harriet Beecher Stowe

135,000 SETS, 270,000 VOLUMES SOLD.

UNCLE TOM'S CABIN

FOR SALE HERE.

AN EDITION FOR THE MILLION, COMPLETE IN 1 Vol. PRICE 37 1-2 CENTS.
" " IN GERMAN, IN 1 Vol. PRICE 50 CENTS.
" " IN 2 Vols. CLOTH, 6 PLATES, PRICE $1.50.
SUPERB ILLUSTRATED EDITION, IN 1 Vol. WITH 153 ENGRAVINGS,
PRICES FROM $2.50 TO $5.00.

The Greatest Book of the Age.

In about 1860 a shopkeeper announces the sale of several editions of Stowe's controversial novel.

23

DRIVING THE UNDERGROUND RAILROAD

Black and white, young and old, male and female all helped to keep the "freight" (runaway slaves) chugging north on the Underground Railroad. These are just a few of the heroes: A tall and dynamic black woman, Sojourner Truth (born Isabella Baumfree) ran away from her New York slave master in the 1820s and became an ardent spokeswoman for the abolitionist movement. Those who dared to challenge her were often stung by her wit. When after a speech, a listener declared, "I don't care any more for your talk than I do for the bite of a flea," Sojourner Truth replied, "Perhaps not... but I'll keep you scratchin'."

Theodore Parker was a white Boston Unitarian minister who urged his parishioners to aid runaway slaves whenever they could. He even hid numbers of slaves himself and got them to Canada. Parker justified his actions on purely religious grounds.

A powerful speaker in behalf of abolition was Charles Lenox Remond, a black man born free in Salem, Massachusetts. A member of the American Anti-Slavery Society, he spent many months in Great Britain and Ireland speaking against the evils of slavery.

Lucretia Mott was a white Quaker minister who founded the Philadelphia Female Anti-Slavery Society in 1833. Said she, "Quakerism does not mean quietism."

The poet John Greenleaf Whittier lent his artistic talents to liberal causes. He wrote hundreds of antislavery poems between 1833 and 1865, ridiculing slavery in many ways by asking such questions as "Is this the land our fathers loved?"

A well-to-do white woman, Maria Chapman of Boston, was certainly no wilting lily. A staunch backer of William Lloyd Garrison, she once attended an antislavery meeting for women when it was surrounded by an unruly mob. Fearing for the safety of the blacks in the group, she urged the white ladies each to take the arm of a black companion. The women marched quietly and safely from the hall and went on to Chapman's home to finish the meeting.

Perhaps the most well-known name in Underground Railroad lore is that of the tiny dynamo Harriet Tubman, an ex-slave who escaped from Maryland in 1849. She was so fearless and so clever at disguise that she was never caught, even though she led some 300 slaves to freedom. They were never caught either. Not even the Civil War stopped her. She served the Union army as a cook, laundress, nurse, and spy.

No one knows how many slaves actually escaped on the Underground Railroad. The numbers vary from about 40,000 to 100,000. In addition to gaining freedom for many, it helped to cause the war in two ways. It caused many Northerners to become sympathetic to the abolitionist movement, and it caused many Southerners to realize that never, never would North and South agree over the issue of slavery.

Levi Coffin's farm in Indiana, a station on the Underground Railroad, welcomes slaves as they head for the Canadian border and freedom.

It's important to remember that not all Southerners, slave owners or not, defended slavery. Some even freed their slaves. Some thought that wrong or not, slavery was not as important an issue as the right of the South to protect its way of life. Others believed that slavery would eventually die out no matter what anyone did.

Perhaps it would have, but when the 1860s began, slavery was a very prickly issue between North and South. Most white Southerners were not about to compromise. Ban slavery? Free the slaves? Most would have been appalled at the mere suggestion that an ex-slave could ever live peacefully among them.

Actually, most white Northerners also probably would have been appalled at the idea of blacks living peacefully among them. The North may have been against slavery as a practice, but few Northerners gave much thought to the slaves as people. Of course, blacks in the North had far greater freedom than blacks

A UNION HERO

The first black staff officer in the U.S. military was Major Martin R. Delany, who entered the army on February 26, 1865. Although he never exercised a field command, Delany was an able recruiter of black soldiers for the Union. After the war he once told an audience, "Do you know that if it was not for the black men this war never would have been brought to a close with success to the Union, and the liberty of your race if it had not been for the Negro? I want you to understand that."

Time and again in battle, the courage of black soldiers won the respect of their white officers.

in the South. They could vote in some states—Maine, Massachusetts, New Hampshire, Rhode Island, and Vermont, for instance. They could serve on juries in most of New England except Connecticut. Generally, most could go to school, own guns, choose a profession, and hold public office. However, Northern black people faced much inequality and prejudice.

They did have the freedom, by the end of 1862, to join the U.S. Army. Most white soldiers—North or South—didn't want to serve with black Americans, however. That attitude began to change somewhat after the fighting began. Brigadier General James G. Blunt said of the lst Kansas Colored Volunteers, who were part of his command, "Their coolness and bravery I have never seen surpassed; they were in the hottest of the fight, and opposed to Texas troops twice their number, whom they completely routed."

So, the nation grew and grew apart, divided by North and South, by white and black, by slave and free. Honest and well-meaning people, as well as some not so honest or well meaning, tried to patch up the differences... a slave state here, a free state there. Put a bandage on this problem, give a poor solution to the next. Nothing really worked. Nothing could work because no one tackled the real problem. As long as there was slavery, there would never be peace. In the end, of course, there was war. But in those last few ticks of the clock before the firing on Fort Sumter in 1861, a few Americans tried to find other ways to keep an ever dividing house together.

The Bandage Compromises, Mexico, and Bleeding Kansas

2

Did you ever cut your arm or leg rather badly? You have an open wound, and you know it's there, but as long as it doesn't bleed too much, you try to forget about it. If it does bleed, you try to stop it with a bandage. Perhaps two bandages. Anything, just as long as you don't have to go to the doctor!

Slavery was like that, a big open wound on the young United States. The years passed and the disharmony over slavery grew right along with the country. Although extremists on both sides were passionate and vocal, most Americans, including the nation's leaders, stuck with the fresh wound policy. If it doesn't bleed, pretend it's not there. If it does bleed, try another bandage. From 1820 until the firing on Fort Sumter in 1861, America's leaders tried a number of bandages to keep the country from sliding into war with itself. Each attempt was an effort by dedicated people to find a fair and workable solution to this nagging problem. But in every case, the result was failure, and the gulf between North and South deepened. The most notable of these failed attempts were the Missouri Compromise, the Compromise of 1850, and the Kansas-Nebraska Act.

As the United States of America was ending its third decade, there were still traces of the mutual sympathy that had existed between North and South during the American Revolution. Some slave owners grumbled about the 1808 ban against African slave trade, but by and large their protests were mild. As were complaints from Northerners about the "peculiar institution" known as slavery. No one knows who coined the term "peculiar institution," but it was sometimes used in the South when referring to slavery. Southerners did not mean to imply that slavery was odd or strange, just that it was unique.

Part of the reason for the good neighbor policy between North and South was the balance of political power. The U.S. Constitution divides the Congress into the House of Representatives, with the number of members based on population, and the Senate, with two members from each state. When Alabama entered the Union in 1819, the total number of states reached 22. More important to the South, exactly 11 were free states and exactly 11 were slave. Since the North had a larger population than the South, it controlled the House of Representatives. But bills in Congress have to be passed by both the House and the Senate. With the Senate evenly divided between slave and nonslave states, the South felt secure in its power to keep antislavery bills from becoming law. Southern senators always voted against antislave laws, but the South could generally count on at least one or two Northern sympathizers to side with it.

Then, along came the question of statehood for the Missouri territory, and the calm was shattered. In fact, the uproar would occupy the Congress for the next two years.

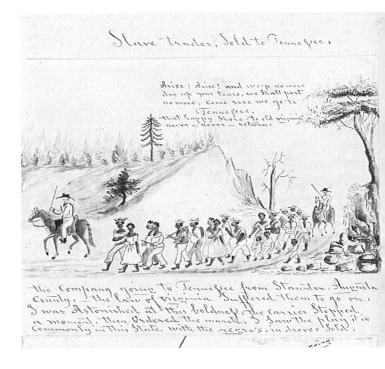

Although foreign trade in slaves became illegal in 1808, internal slave trade flourished. Here, traders take slaves from Virginia to Tennessee for sale.

Back in 1803, President Thomas Jefferson authorized the Louisiana Purchase. It was the greatest land bargain in U.S. history. France sold 828,000 square miles for less than three cents an acre, and the United States doubled in size! When Louisiana became a state in 1812, the rest of the Purchase was known as the Missouri Territory. Seven years later, part of that territory, with 56,000 citizens and 10,000 slaves, wanted to become the state of Missouri.

The North opposed admission because of another slave state in the Union. Also, by law, the South was allowed to count three-fifths of its slaves when determining representation in Congress. The North did not want to see this practice extend farther into the former Louisiana Territory. Naturally, the South was for Missouri's petition.

Into the struggle stepped James Tallmadge, a little-known congressman from New York. On February 13, 1819, he introduced a resolution that shook the Congress and the nation. Former President John Quincy Adams later said it was "a title page to a great tragic volume." The aged Thomas Jefferson said he considered it "at once the knell [meaning death] of the union."

What Tallmadge proposed was this. After Missouri entered the Union, no more slaves would be brought into the state and all slaves then in Missouri would be given their freedom at the age of 25. Naturally, the South was having none of this, and it touched off a nasty debate on the federal government's right to ban slavery in any part of the states.

The Tallmadge proposal did pass the House, which the North controlled, but not the Senate. Even though the Senate was evenly divided between North and South, some Northern senators voted against it. So, this latest challenge to slavery was defeated, and Congress adjourned.

Back in session that December of 1819, Congress was ready to start the fight all over again. But the times had changed. A new territory, Maine, had separated from the state of Massachusetts and applied for statehood. One of America's great political leaders, Henry Clay of Kentucky, now stepped in and earned himself the nickname of "The Great Pacificator." He helped to write the Missouri Compromise of 1820, which declared that Missouri would enter as a slave state and Maine as free. An added provision banned slavery in all other parts of the Louisiana Purchase north of 36 degrees, 30 minutes. In other words, only what would become the states of Arkansas and Oklahoma south of that line could become slave states. In spite of furious opposition on both sides, the moderates won the day and the compromise was passed.

Maine joined the Union in 1820. But before Missouri could be admitted, it had to submit a state constitution to the Congress. The document stated that free blacks from other states could not enter Missouri. That clearly violated the U.S. Constitution, which grants citizens of any state the rights and privileges of other states. According to the Missouri constitution, a free black man in New Jersey, for instance, would not be allowed to cross the boundary into Missouri.

Once again, Clay stepped in, although this time his compromise would prove unacceptable to many. It said that Congress should vote for Missouri's constitution provided that no law passed by its state legislature would ever violate the U.S. Constitution. But, of course, Missouri's constitution already did violate the U.S. Constitution. Nonetheless, when the Congress finally voted, Missouri became a state in 1821.

Known in history for his fine speeches and ability to enact compromises, Henry Clay also proved to be charming, sociable, quick-witted, extremely ambitious, and a gambling man–qualities not unappreciated in Kentucky society.

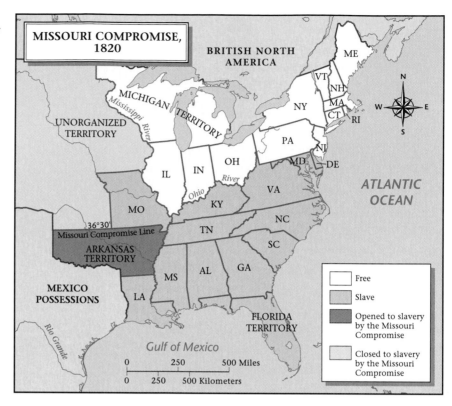

Despite the efforts of Henry Clay and others, this map showing the boundaries of the Missouri Compromise was to become just lines on paper after all.

The Missouri Compromise appeared to have settled the question of spreading slavery in the territories. Although passions did cool somewhat, in reality another bandage had just been put on the open wound. The problem had not been solved at all and would soon flare up again. The Compromise itself would be repealed in 1854 and then declared unconstitutional in 1857.

The Missouri Compromise surely widened the gulf between North and South, but it did African-Americans—both slave and free—no good either. Certainly, in general, blacks fared better in terms of educational and other opportunities in the North than in the South. Yet, the Compromise suddenly made many Northerners face the possibility that slavery might really be eliminated. That would mean that whites and blacks would be equal. That thought was so unsettling to some in the Northern states that they began to look for ways to limit opportunities for free blacks. In Charleston, South Carolina, a freed slave named

Denmark Vesey planned a massive uprising in 1822. He believed that he would be supported by the North. He was not, and he paid for his mistake by being hanged. Southern whites now became more fearful about a major slave revolt. That led to more restrictions than ever on the lives of slaves in the South.

During these troubled times, the growing nation was, of course, involved with other problems, both internal and international. But the ever-widening rift between North and South remained the most important concern. Such ardent abolitionists as William Lloyd Garrison were loud and long in their condemnation of slave owners as criminals. One group, the American Colonization Society, raised money to send freed blacks to an area in West Africa in 1822. The region later became the independent country of Liberia. The Underground Railroad helped thousands of runaway slaves. And in 1831, Nat Turner, a Virginia slave, led others in a savage attack on whites in the area. Some Southerners were terrified that an all-out slave revolt was about to begin.

The Missouri Compromise had seemed to paper over the slavery problem in 1820. But new tensions and political disagreements arose almost immediately and continually. The Nullification Crisis made the South ever more aware of how vulnerable it could be to a Northern majority. Bitter over federal tariffs (taxes), South Carolina adopted an ordinance that declared null and void the tariffs of 1828 and 1832. That meant a state could stop enforcement of a federal law. But President Andrew Jackson proclaimed the supremacy of the federal government and vowed to send in troops if necessary to collect the tariff. South Carolina backed down.

Stands on slavery turned more rigid on both sides. The language became more extreme. What had been half-hidden was now out in the open. Gone was the "gentleman's decision" to look

IN SOLID DEFENSE OF SLAVERY

Slavery, declared John C. Calhoun (1782-1850) of South Carolina, was "a positive good... the most safe and stable basis for free institutions in the world."

James Hammond (1807-1864), also of South Carolina, was unyielding about not freeing the slaves. To do so, he said, would be to "deliberately consign our children [meaning white southern youngsters] to the flames."

Made bold by the fact that he believed he had truth on his side, Senator Robert M.T. Hunter (1809-1887) of Virginia declared that there was not a "respectable system of civilization known to history whose foundations were not laid in the institution of domestic slavery."

the other way. Slavery was evil, shouted the North. Goaded into a defensive position, the South was vocal in justifying it.

This rather tense atmosphere burned slowly until it was given a new spark by the two-year war with Mexico beginning in 1846. The fight was over the boundary line of Texas, which the United States had annexed, and California, a Mexican province that the United States wanted. These moves to expand boundaries were justified by the U.S. idea of "Manifest Destiny." It sounded grand, but what it really said was that Americans now felt they had a "God-given right to take over the North American continent from sea to sea." Supposedly, this phrase, often used by those who favored the idea of American expansion, was coined by John L. O'Sullivan in his *United States Magazine and Democratic Review* (July-August 1845).

Some Southern leaders were agog with the wonderful possibilities of victory in the war with Mexico. Perhaps the whole of Mexico could become part of the United States, meaning new slave states! In 1846, the U.S. stood at 14 slave and 15 free states. Victory over Mexico would be a great boon for the South!

That dream was shattered by a tobacco-chewing lawyer from Pennsylvania named David Wilmot. In 1846, he introduced a bill into Congress declaring no slavery should exist in any territory conquered as a result of the Mexican War. The so-called Wilmot Proviso never passed the Senate, but the damage was done. It was obvious to all that on slavery issues, Congress was no longer voting along party lines, as Democrats or Whigs, the two major political parties of the day, but as Northerners and Southerners. The rift widened.

The war ended in 1848. Mexico did not become part of the United States, but it did lose a third of its territory. In contrast, the United States was suddenly bigger by a newly acquired one million square miles. Immediately the fighting started again in the U.S. Congress over the issue of slavery. By now, tempers were so heated that threats of dissolving the Union were almost commonplace. But few really believed it would happen. This was just spirited talk.

Then, along came more trouble. This time, the bandage was needed for California.

By late 1849, California, thanks to the discovery of gold near Sutters Mill, just outside of Sacramento, now the state capital, was booming. It, along with the territory of New Mexico, was about to apply for statehood. Up popped the old issue of slavery. The North said both territories should be

AN ARMY OF WHITES ONLY

When the Civil War began, a few hundred Mexican-Americans, mainly in Texas, Colorado, and New Mexico, took up arms for the North. But they were so poorly treated or ignored by Federal commanders that many of them just left the army or joined the Rebels. Native Americans fared little better. About 4,000 fought for the Union and more than 10,000 joined the Confederacy—Seminole, Cherokee, Chickasaw, and others. In total, they made up some 11 regiments and acquitted themselves well in battle. White soldiers often complained, however, that the Native American "dressed up" his uniform with silver earrings or a feathered headband.

NOT MUCH OF A SCHOLAR

Winfield Scott, Lincoln's general in charge of the Union forces at the start of the Civil War, apparently did not have a high opinion of Zachary Taylor. That may have been because they had been rivals for the 1848 presidential nomination, which Scott lost. In any case, Scott is said to have remarked: "General Taylor's mind had not been enlarged and refreshed by reading, or much converse with the world.... In short, few men have ever had a more comfortable, labor-saving contempt for learning of every kind."

People took note of General Winfield Scott, for his proven military talents and also for his formidable 300-plus pounds.

organized without slavery, according to the Wilmot Proviso, or at the very least, the people living there should be the ones to decide the issue. The South disagreed.

Sitting in the White House at the time was the twelfth President of the United States, "Old Rough and Ready" Zachary Taylor, ex-general, popular hero of the Mexican War, and slave owner. Taylor may have been well intentioned, but he was woefully inexperienced in the ways of politics.

He thought he could solve the slavery issue and save the Union. He couldn't and didn't.

Moderates in Congress decided that California should be admitted as a state without the in-between and usual step of first forming a territorial government. In that way, they thought, they could skirt the slavery issue. President Taylor agreed. If California were a state, its citizens instead of Congress could decide the fate of slavery. In November 1849, California asked to be admitted as a free state.

The Union might have ended right there! The South was outraged! How dare the president—a Southerner at that—favor such a trick! California would upset the delicate balance between slave and free. It seemed for sure that this time the walls of

Congress would come tumbling down. Southern extremists had been demanding for years that the South leave the Union, and now the shout was heard again.

The Civil War might well have started 11 years before it did had it not been for some dedicated leaders of experience and goodwill who made one more try to keep the dividing house together. The most outstanding of these men was Henry Clay, the Great Compromiser, now in his seventies and ill.

Clay well knew how close the country was to splitting apart. He believed that California would enter as a free state. But he felt that the South had to be given some concessions. And so, with the backing of such leaders as Daniel Webster and Stephen Douglas, Clay proposed what became the Compromise of 1850.

California would enter the Union as a free state. Texas would get some of the lands known as New Mexico. The rest of New Mexico and Utah would be formed as territories, and the people themselves would decide the slavery issue.

Clay's proposals brought on a magnificent seven-month debate in the United States Senate as three giants—perhaps the greatest senators ever to sit in that esteemed body—presented their solutions. In faltering voice, the gravely ill Clay appealed to the South for peace and to the North for concessions. His opponent, John C. Calhoun of South Carolina, himself too ill to deliver his own speech, implored his fellow senators to "let the

General Zachary Taylor had spent 38 years in the army before becoming President of the United States in 1849.

37

In what was to be the last great chance to save the Union, the giants of the U.S. Congress step into their finest hour. Here, 72-year-old Henry Clay implores his colleagues to resolve their differences.

states... agree to separate and part in peace... If you are unwilling... tell us so, and we shall know what to do, when you reduce the question to submission or resistance."

Into the deadlock stepped statesman Daniel Webster for his last great speech. His powerful voice now weak and hesitant, he hushed the Senate galleries with his opening words: "I speak today for the preservation of the Union. Hear me for my cause."

And so they did. The debate would go on for months, but Webster had brought back, for a time at least, a willingness to compromise.

Still, the stalemate and debate in Congress continued. Not that President Taylor was much help. He would not listen to any attempts, no matter how mild, that would change his plan to have California and New Mexico enter the Union without any direction from Congress. Taylor went so far as to declare that if the South seceded, he would personally lead the U.S. Army to put down such a rebellion.

Unfortunately for Taylor, he attended ceremonies at the unfinished Washington Monument on July 4, 1850, a hot and sunny day. Consuming vast amounts of cherries and cold milk apparently brought on an acute stomach disorder. President Taylor died suddenly on July 8, 1850. His vice president, Millard Fillmore of New York, who was a bit more moderate in his policies, ended the stalemate between White House and Congress. The Compromise of 1850 was passed and Fillmore signed it into law. It really wasn't much of a bandage, but it was enough to keep the Union together—for one more decade... and just barely.

Those ten years, however, would make a huge difference in the eventual outcome of the Civil War. The North had experienced tremendous growth in population during this period. Its manufacturing capacity had vastly improved. More and more Northern cities were being joined by rail lines to carry the goods from the North's expanding factories. These factors would give the North a tremendous advantage when it began to mobilize for war.

Although few people were jumping up and down with glee over the 1850 compromise, both sides at least showed some willingness to back it in an effort to reduce some of the tension. In fact, the election of 1852 was won by a little-known Democrat,

THE ELOQUENT OLD MAN

Speaking with an eloquence rarely heard in the halls of Congress, or anywhere, Daniel Webster's Seventh of March speech, 1850, called for the best in his countrymen with these words: "Peaceable secession! Heaven forbid! Where is the flag of the republic to remain? Where is the eagle still to tower!"

THE FUGITIVE SLAVE ACT, 1850

Part of the Compromise of 1850 was the extremely harsh Fugitive Slave Act. It said that federal marshals could compel ordinary citizens to hunt down fugitives, that people accused of being slaves could be sent back to the South without trial, and that a person arrested as an escaped slave could not testify in his or her own defense. Since relatively few slaves—about 1,000 a year—ever did escape and because the law was so difficult to enforce, only about 360 slaves were returned to their owners under this law. It did, however, increase the already strained relations between North and South on slavery.

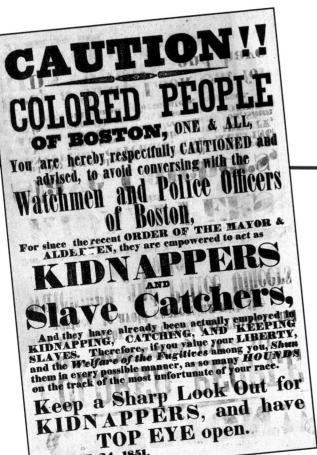

Some Northerners, like those who posted this notice in Boston, reacted to the Fugitive Slave Act by warning blacks to watch out for policemen and others who might turn them in.

well-meaning Franklin Pierce of New Hampshire, mainly because he seemed more enthusiastic over the Compromise of 1850 than did the Whig candidate, General Winfield Scott.

The 1852 election signaled the death not only of Scott's presidential ambitions, but of the party itself. It never again ran a candidate for president and, in fact, would go out of existence a few years later, to be replaced by what is now the other major political party in the United States, the Republicans.

Sometimes, if you have a flat desk and a steady hand, you can balance a nickel on end for a very long time. It will just stay there, caught between standing and falling. At least until a gust of wind blows in, or someone slams a door. The North and the South were like the two sides of that nickel, just staying there, caught between war and peace. Then, along came Kansas and slammed the door.

Now it was 1854; seven years before the house would divide in earnest. Franklin Pierce was entering his second year in the White House. Just 49 years old when he took office, he was the youngest president elected thus far. In addition, some say he was one of the handsomest. It is unfortunate they couldn't also say he was one of the most decisive or able. To be sure, the President was in a sticky position in 1854, but he was often paralyzed because he couldn't make up his mind. He understood that war could be averted only by compromise, but he often bent over backward to favor the South. It did not work, and Kansas became

OLD FUSS AND FEATHERS

General Winfield Scott, a great mountain of a man, earned the nickname "Old Fuss and Feathers" because he was extremely vain and always nagging about something. A Virginian, he would remain loyal to the Union during the Civil War. "I fought 50 years under the flag," he said, "and would fight for it, and under it, till death."

the great tragedy of Pierce's administration. Not only did it cost him control of his own party and give the new antislavery Republican party a foothold in government, but it was the last big push on the slide to war.

Early in January 1854, Senator Stephen A. Douglas of Illinois introduced a bill to organize the Nebraska Territory, which included Kansas, in preparation for statehood. Douglas, known as the Little Giant because he was short but had a most imposing voice, saw Kansas as a railroad passage from the West Coast right to his native state.

There were two potential problems with Douglas's proposal. The first was that organizing the new territory would mean breaking several treaties the government now held with Native-American tribes. As might be imagined, some congressmen saw little trouble getting around that. But the second problem was serious; slavery, of course. The new territory was north of the

New boundaries are drawn from the Kansas-Nebraska Act of 1854.

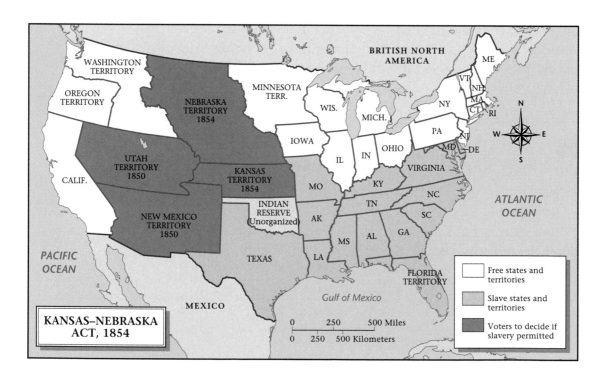

Missouri Compromise line. And, according to the Missouri Compromise, that meant there could be no slavery in the new states. Naturally, the South was not going to agree to that. In fact, Missouri Senator David R. Atchison had stated that he would "sink in hell" before he saw Kansas enter the Union as a free state.

Undaunted, Douglas had a new plan. Now he proposed that the bill would allow the people of Nebraska and Kansas to settle the slavery question themselves once the areas became states. That meant that they might very well become slave states. But the Missouri Compromise had already declared no slavery in those lands. Wouldn't this new bill destroy the Compromise?

Free-state partisans in Kansas Territory stand ready to fight slave-state forces in what would become a series of bloody battles.

The South thought so. At any rate, the Kansas-Nebraska Act of 1854 was passed, and the President went along with it. All the old wounds closed by the Missouri Compromise were opened once again. The public was outraged. Douglas was nearly mobbed and killed in his own state. Of the 42 Northern Democrats who voted for the bill, only seven were re-elected. Pierce was without control of his own party. Of course, some congressmen saw things in another light. Charles Sumner of Massachusetts said this was the "best bill on which Congress ever acted" because it "makes all future compromises impossible."

Even so, that wasn't the end of it. Missouri might have become a slave state, but the North was not about to let Kansas follow. Soon the territory became the scene of a bitter mini-civil war. Antislavery settlers flocked in from New England and proslavery champions flooded in from Missouri and states to the south.

The territory's first election was held on March 30, 1855.

Ferrying proslavery Missouri voters into Kansas became one method of assuring victory for the spread of slavery.

According to the census taken, just 2,905 men were eligible to vote, most of them from the North. But when the ballots were counted, the total number of votes was 6,307, a majority of them for slavery! Obviously, there had been some illegal voting. But when Andrew H. Reeder, sent to Kansas by Pierce as the territorial governor, attempted to disqualify some of these irregular votes, the South screamed no. Pierce caved in and he refused to back his own governor. The illegally elected government stayed in office and set up a capital at Lecompton. Reeder, fearing he would be killed otherwise, recognized this government, forcing Pierce to do so as well. And when the new government told Pierce to remove Reeder and put William Shannon of Ohio in as the governor, the President did that, too.

The antislavery side in Kansas was not backing down, however. They held their own convention, wrote a constitution that banned slavery, set up a government in Topeka, and named Charles Robinson as governor.

Just what Pierce needed! Kansas now had two governors, two legislatures, and two capitals. While the President pondered a decision, fighting broke out and more than 200 men died in the territory in 1856. Involved in one attack against the proslavery group was fanatical John Brown, whose name would later become a rallying cry for some in the North. From these bitter and deadly battles came the name of Bleeding Kansas.

In the meantime, Pierce appointed yet another governor for Kansas, John W. Geary. He was able to obtain some appearance of peace, but once again it was a bandage covering another deep and unhealing wound. Bleeding Kansas was simply the last straw. There would be, as Senator Sumner had said, no further compromises. Kansas did finally enter the Union in 1861. It became the thirty-fourth state, and it was free.

How wide and quarrelsome the rift over slavery had grown was evident in a new lack of dignity in Congress. This was no longer a "let's shake hands and act like gentlemen group." Senators and representatives began to carry pistols and knives into the hallowed halls in fear for their own safety. Ever vocal Charles Sumner ranted loud and long against the evils of slavery, at one point attacking Andrew Butler of South Carolina, who he said "has chosen a mistress... who although ugly to others is always lovely to him... I mean the harlot Slavery."

The elderly Senator Butler was not in the Senate chamber at the time of Sumner's speech. However, a few days later, Butler's nephew, Congressman Preston Brooks, strode into the Senate and approached Sumner from behind as he was seated at his desk. "... you have libelled my State and slandered my white haired old relative," he declared. With that, he began hitting Sumner over the head with a cane. Sumner could not defend himself and was injured so badly that he did not return to the Senate for two years. Brooks resigned for his actions, but was reelected almost unanimously in November 1856.

The decade was coming to a close, and war was coming closer.

Dred Scott and John Brown

3

Dred Scott, the mild-mannered slave whose quest for freedom became a giant step toward war.

Would there have been a civil war without Dred Scott and John Brown? Almost surely. But did these incidents—one involving a black man and one a white—widen the gulf between North and South? Absolutely. And in the case of John Brown, the uproar over his hanging increased the fear and hatred between North and South to the point of no return. Many Americans began to feel that there was nowhere left to go but the battlefield.

Dred Scott was a black man and a slave. Born in Virginia, he was eventually sold to Dr. John Emerson of St. Louis, Missouri. In 1834, Emerson, a brand new army surgeon, reported for duty at Rock Island in Illinois, which was not a slave state. The doctor took Scott with him. Two years later, Scott went with Emerson to Fort Snelling in Wisconsin Territory (present-day Minnesota). Slavery was outlawed there, too. At Fort Snelling, Scott married Harriet Robinson, who also became Emerson's property.

Master and slaves returned to Missouri in 1838, and the surgeon died five years later. Both Dred and Harriet Scott remained in service to Emerson's wife. Scott sued Irene Emerson for his and his wife's freedom in 1846. The argument was that Scott's years in a free state and territory had made him free. and in 1850, the St. Louis Circuit Court declared him free. His freedom was short-lived, however, for two years later the Missouri Supreme Court reversed the lower court's decision. Once more Scott was declared a slave.

Although not free, in the meantime Dred Scott's life had changed. His new owner was John F.A. Sanford, a New Yorker and Mrs. Emerson's brother. She had remarried and moved to New England. Because Sanford lived outside Missouri, Scott's case could now be argued in the federal district court, which ruled over interstate matters. And in this manner, in 1857, the fate of Dred Scott rested in the minds of the men who sat on the U.S. Supreme Court. With the Court's decision, the name of the slave Dred Scott was forever linked with the name of Supreme Court Chief Justice Roger Brooke Taney.

Taney (1777-1864) was the Court's fifth Chief Justice, appointed in 1835 after the death of John Marshall. A deeply religious Roman Catholic, the Maryland-born Taney had freed his own slaves when he was a young man, but over the years he had grown increasingly racist in outlook.

The U.S. Supreme Court was now faced with a prickly two-pronged problem. Did Dred Scott, a slave, have the right to sue in federal court? Or, was he a free man because he had lived in the Wisconsin Territory, in which the Missouri Compromise had outlawed slavery?

The Court's opinion was delivered on March 6, 1857, and went down in

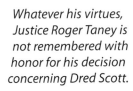

A LINK TO THE ANTHEM

Chief Justice Taney was the son of wealthy tobacco growers. He was educated at Dickinson College in Pennsylvania and became a lawyer in 1799. Seven years later, he married Anne Key. Her brother, Francis Scott Key, wrote "The Star Spangled Banner" in 1814.

Whatever his virtues, Justice Roger Taney is not remembered with honor for his decision concerning Dred Scott.

history as the Dred Scott Decision. Voting seven to two, the U.S. Supreme Court, led by Chief Justice Roger B. Taney, decided against Scott.

Speaking for the Court, Taney declared that Dred Scott was still a slave on several counts. He was a black, which meant he was not a citizen of the United States and therefore was not entitled to the rights of citizenship. In other words, Scott had no right to sue in the first place. The Court also declared that Scott was still a slave because he had never been free. Congress, said the Court, could not prohibit slavery in territories such as Wisconsin because the Constitution did not give it such power. This decision, of course, neatly wiped out the Missouri Compromise.

Scott had lost, and the South had won. Or had it? The reaction to the Court's decision was immediate and outspoken. Free states were outraged! They feared the next step would be to make slavery legal everywhere. Taney, said the press, was a man of "wicked judgment."

THE WORST DECISION IN U.S. SUPREME COURT HISTORY!

Today, constitutional scholars declare the decision in the Dred Scott case to be the worst in Supreme Court history. But even back in 1857, people were outraged. Many in the North were shocked! Its citizens were even more upset when Taney argued that at the time the Constitution was adopted, blacks were universally considered "beings of an inferior order, and altogether unfit to associate with the white race, either in social or political relations, and so far inferior, that they had no rights which the white man was bound to respect; and that the negro might justly and lawfully be reduced to slavery for his [white people's] benefit."

In the Dred Scott case, the Court had gone beyond the immediate case and handed down broad principles that created great turmoil in the nation. It would take two Constitutional amendments to undue the Dred Scott decision. The Thirteenth Amendment abolished slavery in 1865. Three years later, the Fourteenth Amendment declared that all those born in the United States, regardless of color or previous slave condition, were U.S. citizens, with all the rights thereof.

Dred Scott himself, who died in 1858, did not live to see those changes in the U.S. Constitution. In a sense, however, he won his own case because, after Sanford's death, his new owner granted freedom to Scott, his wife, and their two daughters, Eliza and Lizzie, on May 26, 1857.

As it concerns the Civil War, the Dred Scott case had a profound influence. It caused many fair-minded people on both sides of the issue to believe that any compromise over slavery between North and South was now impossible.

The country had moved another step closer to disaster. But if Dred Scott was a step, surely John Brown was a leap. And what a strange figure he was! John Brown was a militant abolitionist with a deep and bitter hatred of slavery. Many said he was a murderer and a madman. Some members of his own family claimed he was crazy and should be put into an institution. Others said he was a saint. Evidence suggests that he was not actually insane, but such was his faith in his cause that the name of John Brown is forever linked to the start of the American Civil War. With his death, he became a symbol of noncompromise between North and South.

John Brown was born in Torrington, Connecticut, on May 9, 1800. Five years later his father moved the family to Hudson, Ohio. At first it was a hard life, clearing land and building a cabin. Then tragedy struck with the death of his mother in 1808. Nevertheless, Brown went to school and prepared for college in

John Brown, one of the nation's more perplexing figures: militant abolitionist and fanatic to be sure; madman as well?

Massachusetts and Connecticut. As a grown man, Brown was an impressive, somewhat startling figure. He stood stiff and straight, appearing taller than his actual five feet nine. He had bushy eyebrows and a penetrating stare. Some said his lean, leathery face looked like an eagle's. One of his sons said he looked more like a meat axe.

Like his father, Brown worked at several different trades to support his numerous children. Sometimes he was a farmer, sometimes a wool merchant, sometimes a leather tanner. He also inherited his father's fierce hatred of slavery. As the years passed, more and more he believed himself to be "God's agent on earth," speaking angrily against slave owners, whom he referred to as "Satan and his legions." Brown earned a reputation as a fanatic on the subject of slavery, but he was impressive when he cried out against its evils. People couldn't help but notice him.

Although he was white, Brown took his family to North Elba, New York, in 1849, and settled in that free black farming community. There, he became obsessed with the idea of "doing something" that would end slavery. Six years later, he followed five of his sons to the Kansas Territory. The region was in the midst of a bitter struggle between proslavery and antislavery factions. Taking along a wagonload of guns and ammunition, Brown settled in Osawatomie near the Pottawatomie Creek.

In the spring of 1856, Brown grew despondent after hearing that the town of Lawrence, Kansas, had been attacked by a mob of proslavery sympathizers. This was the time, he decided. His "divine mission" was clear.

It was all too clear around midnight, May 24, 1856. Pleasant

Doyle, a proslavery supporter, answered a knock on his cabin door on Pottawatomie Creek. Five men stood there. They dragged Doyle and two of his sons outside, sparing Doyle's wife and 14-year-old son. The three Doyles were hacked to death.

The killing spree did not end there. Down the road from the Doyles lived Allen Wilkinson, another proslavery supporter, and his wife. Again, the male victim was dragged outside and murdered.

From there, it was on to a saloonkeeper, "Dutch Henry" Sherman. Luckily for Dutch Henry, he wasn't home. Unluckily for brother Bill, he was. Brown and his sons split the man's skull.

"Old Osawatomie Brown" had made a statement.

There was not any doubt who was responsible for the Pottawatomie Creek massacre. In fact, Doyle's son and Wilkinson's wife later identified Brown. But Brown was never arrested. Some newspapers in the east hinted that perhaps the murders had never taken place at all. Others hinted that perhaps the killers were only protecting themselves. It was only years later that the true facts about the massacre became known.

Brown, of course, would not have called it a massacre, but an execution. For this was a brutal guerrilla war with much violence on both sides. For instance, a Baptist minister would later shoot one of Brown's sons at point blank range. The young man was unarmed at the time.

John Brown stayed out of the spotlight for a while, trying to raise money for his cause. By 1858, he came up with a new idea. He would establish a stronghold in the Allegheny Mountains. From there he would invade Virginia, free slaves, and bring them back to his headquarters where they would be trained into a fighting army. Then they would take over the South. Brown had not the slightest doubt that once slaves heard of this new army, they would escape from every state and join him. "When I strike," he said, "the bees will swarm."

Before that happened, Brown had yet another scheme. He was going to steal supplies for his army by taking over the Harpers Ferry, Virginia (now West Virginia), federal arsenal. So it was that, on the night of October 16, 1859, with an army of 16 whites, four free blacks, and one escaped slave, John Brown led the raid on the Harpers Ferry arsenal.

For such a wild scheme, everything was remarkably easy. Perhaps the arsenal guards were simply shocked senseless by the sight of a wild-eyed man riding in a wagon who told them he was freeing all the blacks in the state.

Brown and his men took some hostages, including the great-grandnephew of George Washington. Colonel Lewis Washington had a sword that was given to Washington by Frederick the Great of Prussia. Brown strapped it on and walked about the arsenal waiting for all the slaves to come.

Nobody came except several militia companies who finally arrived on October 17. By that time Brown and his followers were in a shooting battle with the townspeople. Now the fighting really turned fierce. Brown, who had made no plans in the event something went wrong, became paralyzed with indecision. Two of his sons, Oliver and Watson, were mortally wounded and in agony. Said Brown, "Die like a man." They did. Actually, Watson was shot while trying to negotiate with the townspeople under a white flag of truce.

By the next morning a company of U.S. Marines had arrived. They were led by Lieutenant Colonel Robert E. Lee of Virginia. When the order came from Washington to retake the arsenal, Lee was home on leave. He had no time to get into uniform so he arrived for battle in civilian clothes.

Lee sent Lieutenant James Ewell Brown (Jeb) Stuart into the arsenal with a white flag and a promise to protect the raiders. Brown, who had seen his son shot while under a white flag, was

determined to keep fighting. But when he was badly wounded by a slashing sword, he surrendered. Only Brown and four of his band lived. One U.S. marine died, as did four townspeople and two slaves. The first of Brown's men killed was Dangerfield Newby, a free black man.

The U.S. government turned Brown over to Virginia to be tried for treason against the state. It was certainly obvious that John Brown was guilty of murder. Who would argue with that? Even those Northerners who loathed the institution of slavery knew that what the fanatical Brown had set out to do was wrong. So, why did John Brown's raid become the last straw in the race to war?

The answer lay in the reaction of the American people. The trial started just ten days after the raid. It lasted for a week. Brown watched the proceedings from a cot carried into the courthouse at Charles Town, Virginia. Everyone knew what the verdict would be. Brown must hang. And so he did, on December 2, 1859.

With the help of John Brown, the little known federal arsenal at Harper's Ferry, shown here, became the new hot spot on the road to war.

That was not the end of this tragic story, however, for Brown's death did what his life could not. It inspired respect and admiration. At his trial, the wild-eyed fanatic had been replaced by a calm, dignified speaker who was passionate in the cause against slavery. At the end of the trial, he said, "... if it is deemed necessary that I should forfeit my life for the furtherance of the ends of justice, and mingle my blood further with the blood of my children and with the blood of millions in this slave country whose rights are disregarded by wicked, cruel, and unjust enactments, I say, let it be done."

Such words and his manner caused many Northerners to praise the man while condemning his actions. The noted abolitionist Reverend Henry Ward Beecher said of Brown, "His soul was noble; his work miserable." The North voiced other

Where has the wild-eyed fanatic gone? A calm, almost dignified John Brown leaves his cot to speak at his trial.

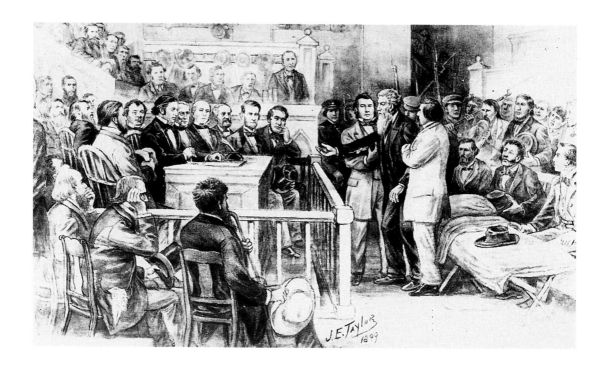

grievances. Brown had been sent to trial before he had recovered from his wounds. The Virginia judge was in such a rush that the trial began before Brown's attorneys arrived. Some thought Brown insane and therefore should not have been hanged at all. So, in hanging Brown, the state of Virginia made him a martyr. He became a hero to millions in the North. The song "John Brown's body lies a'mouldering in the grave" became a marching song for U.S. soldiers when the war started.

But the South was appalled... and afraid. It was one thing for well-known abolitionists like Beecher to praise Brown; it was quite another for the average Northerner to do so. Southerners were terrified that such growing sentiments might bring about what they dreaded most—an overall slave rebellion. Even pro-Union Southerners began to feel that there could be no compromise on this issue between the two sides. By his death, Brown had managed to harden the resolve of both North and South on the issue of slavery.

When Brown climbed the steps of the scaffold to his death that December day in 1859, he handed the guard a note. It read: "I John Brown am now quite certain that the crimes of this guilty land will never be purged away but with blood."

And he was right.

The Election of Abraham Lincoln

Most of us know at least three things about Abraham Lincoln, for sure. He was born in a log cabin, he freed the slaves, and he was an honest man. We should also know that he was totally dedicated to preserving the Union. How strange, then, that Lincoln should be the president whose election caused his beloved Union to divide.

When Abraham Lincoln was elected the sixteenth President of the United States in November 1860, the Union boasted 33 states. But by the time of Lincoln's inauguration in March 1861, there were just 27 states in the not-so-united country. By June, the Union would be divided and the Confederacy formed. It was a sad and deeply troubled time for this President as he watched seemingly helpless and unable to stop the destruction. What could he have thought as he stood in his new home, the White House? Although he surely did not need the reminder, the new President could see from his windows that Rebel flags were fluttering across the Potomac River.

Why was this man of peace a major cause of war?

Perhaps the answer is best illustrated by a Lincoln pledge before his election and the reaction of Southern leaders. Lincoln, a man of moderate antislavery views, swore that as President, he would halt the further spread of slavery. "On that point, hold firm," he told his supporters, "as with a chain of steel. The tug has to come, and better now than any time hereafter."

South Carolina reacted by stating that it would secede from the Union if a president holding such a view were elected. He was, and it did.

War was a likely proposition no matter who occupied the White House, but why pick Abraham Lincoln anyway? Who was he?

He was a 51-year-old lawyer from Illinois, a former congressman who two years earlier had lost a Senate race to the well-known Stephen A. Douglas. The two candidates had argued about slavery and the Kansas issue up and down the state of Illinois, with Douglas winning the Senate seat if not the debates.

What Lincoln was not was his party's first choice. The Republicans picked him over more famous candidates mainly because he held moderate views on slavery. The young party figured that only a moderate could win in this year of great turmoil.

Abraham Lincoln was little known in the East when he was picked to run for the presidency. However, he had already made a name for himself in Illinois. Lincoln was born in the backwoods of Kentucky on February 12, 1809, but his father, who never learned to read and write, moved the family to Indiana and then to Illinois in 1830. Young Abe grew tall and lanky, moody but good-natured. He never received much formal schooling, later saying he had gone to school "by littles"—a little now and a little then. All in all, he probably received the equivalent of one year's formal education. But he taught himself grammar and math and then the law. He passed the bar exam and became a practicing lawyer in 1836.

Lincoln spent six years in the Illinois State Legislature, 1834-1840, as a member of the Whig party. Although he was against slavery—"...it is founded on

Early portraits of Lincoln often idealize his humble beginnings, as in this wood-chopping scene.

injustice and bad policy"—he wasn't fanatic about it. In fact, he said that antislavery legislation only increased its evils.

After one term in the U.S. House of Representatives (1847-1849), Lincoln returned to Illinois with his political career seemingly over. He had criticized the war with Mexico, which did not make him popular with the folks back home. So, he was out of a job, although he did not leave the Whig party until 1854. The Whig party had started to fade after Millard Fillmore became President following Zachary Taylor's death in 1850. By 1856, a new political group had emerged, which Lincoln joined. United against the spread of slavery, party members called themselves Republicans.

According to tradition, the Republican party was born in Ripon, Wisconsin, in 1854. A small group of Whigs who were antislavery met with a group of Democrats, all opposed to the Kansas-Nebraska bill introduced by Senator Douglas. In the election of 1856, the Republicans nominated John C. Frémont, a political newcomer. Although he lost to Democrat James Buchanan, the new party showed surprising strength. In fact, the Republicans captured 11 Northern states.

With the election over, the country looked to cooling tempers over the slavery issue. But before long, it was clear that President Buchanan was not a wound healer. That, coupled with the Supreme Court decision over the slave Dred Scott, only made things worse. By 1858, the Republicans were ready to upset the favorites in the upcoming congressional elections.

Into this charged atmosphere stepped Lincoln. He took on none other than the powerful Little Giant himself, Senator Stephen A. Douglas. Accepting the Republican nomination for the Senate race in June 1858, Lincoln delivered what would become one of his most famous speeches. He declared: "A house divided against itself cannot stand. I believe this government

cannot endure, permanently half slave and half free. I do not expect the Union to be dissolved—I do not expect the house to fall—but I do expect it will cease to be divided. It will become all one thing or all the other."

Thus began one of the most famous political debates in American history. These two men, one a national figure, one little known, both powerful speakers and passionate about their beliefs, began to trek up and down the state of Illinois. If Douglas spoke before a crowd at a small town courthouse, Lincoln appeared on the same steps the very next day to attack his opponent. The crowds grew.

Annoyed with the attention to Lincoln, Douglas's followers charged that the Republican was following the senator because he couldn't draw crowds on his own. In response, Lincoln challenged

The Lincoln-Douglas speeches, this one showing young Lincoln at the podium, go down in U.S. history as perhaps the most famous of all political debates.

Douglas to face-to-face debates. Despite the fact that Douglas was far better known, despite the fact that debates would give attention to a more obscure candidate, the senator's ego may have gotten the better of him. Douglas agreed to seven debates. In so doing, he catapulted Abraham Lincoln right into the national spotlight.

The debates were memorable. In towns such as Freeport and Quincy, large crowds gathered as the entire country became caught up in this contest of beliefs. Douglas never wavered from his theme. Government, he said, "was established upon the white basis. It was made by white men, for the benefit of white men." Although he did not feel that blacks had to be slaves, he did feel that the decision was up to white people. Douglas warned that electing Lincoln would mean political and social equality for blacks.

In response, Lincoln was not for abolishing slavery at all costs. In fact, he sometimes seemed to sit on both sides of the fence. He sometimes appeared to be both antislavery and antiblack. In one speech, he said he was not for social equality. He was not for blacks holding political office, or voting, or, of course, intermarrying. However, in another speech, he said that blacks should have "all the natural rights enumerated in the Declaration of Independence."

Lincoln's beliefs about slavery were both complicated and practical. He truly regarded slavery as evil. Yet he did not believe in fighting it where it already existed as long as slavery did not spread to new territories. Why? Lincoln felt that if slavery were not allowed to spread, it would eventually die out. If it spread, however, it would destroy the Union. Above all, Lincoln stood for preserving the Union.

Poking fun at political opponents is a time-honored tradition. This example is rather gentle, reminding voters of Lincoln's background as a rail splitter.

He lost the election though, and Douglas went back to the Senate by a narrow margin. But Lincoln gained stature. For now, the lanky lawyer from Illinois, with the craggy face and the twang in his voice, was on his way to becoming a national figure.

That happened two years later. It was a snowy night in New York City on February 27, 1860. Some 1,500 New Yorkers had gathered in Cooper Union, an institution for the arts and applied sciences.

They were waiting to hear a politician from Illinois. Although the speaker had been getting some attention over the past two years, these easterners were not usually impressed by "men of the West." Lincoln, after all, did not cut much of a figure in his badly fitting suit and, to them, odd manner of speech. But they were polite if nothing else, and so they listened.

Lincoln was obviously nervous at first. Then he got to the subject of slavery, and his words took on fire as he explained his position. Slavery was a dreadful wrong, he declared. He acknowledged that his party, if elected, would not interfere in the business of slave states. However, he said that the South wanted more than to be left alone. The South wanted the Northern free states to recognize the legitimacy of slavery. Then he asked his audience, "Can we cast our votes with their view, and against our own?... If our sense of duty forbids this, then let us stand by our duty fearlessly and effectively.... Let us have faith that right makes might, and in that faith let us, to the end, dare to do our duty as we understand it."

This speech was remembered by many three months later when the Republicans met in Chicago to choose a presidential candidate. Lincoln was by now at least fairly well known, but he was far from the favorite. The front runner was William Seward of New York, and there were several others with better credentials than Lincoln. Although he realized he was nobody's first choice, Lincoln felt he had a chance if he sat back and let the others cancel themselves out of the race. It worked on the third ballot. Honest Abe became the Republican nominee.

Meanwhile, the Democrats were in deep trouble. They had to find a candidate who would appeal to just about everybody. Since this is impossible at any time, they were unsuccessful. In fact, they could not even come close with a party so divided. At the Democratic convention in Charleston, South Carolina, eight Southern states walked out over the majority refusal to endorse slavery. Those eight put up their own candidate, John C. Breckinridge of Kentucky. The official Democratic candidate was the old warhorse, Stephen Douglas of Illinois. To complicate matters, John Bell of Tennessee, another Democrat, became the nominee of the new National Constitution Union party. This was made up of the remains of the old Whig party, but no one, least of all the voters, seemed quite sure of what it stood for. And just to confuse Democratic voters a little more, Lincoln's running mate was Hannibal Hamlin of Maine. Hamlin was an ex-Democrat.

In a no-nonsense campaign poster of 1860, Honest Abe and ex-Democrat Hamlin urge voters to back the Republicans.

The campaign was spirited if not inspired. Douglas, the experienced campaigner, stomped up and down the country delivering his message. This was, in fact, the first time in presidential election history that a candidate had conducted a campaign in that manner, giving rise to the strange-sounding expression, "going on the stump." Lincoln, in contrast, did not campaign much at all. In fact, he made no speeches. Party leaders were concerned that his attitude about slavery might confuse voters. Instead, the Republicans presented the by now politically experienced lawyer as a patriotic, humble, homespun man of the soil who was willing to give up everything, including the farm, to save his country.

The Democrats, of course, were not above a little misleading of their own. Elect Lincoln, they warned, and private property, states' rights, and freedom itself would go out the window. More serious perhaps were the warnings from the South about leaving the Union if Lincoln got the White House. Lincoln himself thought the warnings were merely a bluff.

The election was held on November 6, 1860. Lincoln was not on the ballot at all in the Deep South, although he did get some votes in Kentucky, Maryland, and Missouri. His three opponents had, among them, about a million votes more than the winner. But, of course, for the Democrats, that was the problem. There were three of them, splitting the vote.

Thus Abraham Lincoln of Illinois became the sixteenth President of the United States. He carried all 18 free states and won a decisive vote in the electoral college, 180 votes to 123 cast for his opponents. The Democratic vote was split between Douglas, who believed in popular sovereignty, the principle that people of the individual states should decide the slavery issue within the state, and Breckinridge, who represented the Southern Democrats and took electoral votes in 11 states from Delaware to

Texas. Douglas won electoral votes in Missouri and New Jersey, though he had 500,000 more popular votes than Breckinridge. Bell took electoral votes in Virginia, Kentucky, and Tennessee.

The Republicans were joyous over the election, but they had very little time to enjoy victory. Ominous signs were emerging from the southland. While Northerners cheered, Southerners burned pictures of the president-elect on courthouse steps. Southern newspapers voiced the general dismay. "The revolution has been initiated," proclaimed the Charleston *Mercury*. Lincoln's election, said the Richmond, Virginia, *Whig*, "is the greatest evil that has ever befallen this country." The New Orleans *Daily Crescent* was even more outraged: "They have robbed us of our property... and finally they have capped the mighty pyramid of unfraternal enormities by electing Abraham Lincoln... on a platform and by a system which indicates nothing but the subjugation of the South and the complete ruin of her social, political and industrial institutions."

Nowhere was this anti-Lincoln feeling more intense than in South Carolina. The state had said it would leave the Union if Lincoln were elected. He was, on November 6, and South Carolina did, on December 20. A state convention called shortly after the election declared that "the union now subsisting between South Carolina and other States under the name of the United States of America is hereby dissolved."

DIRE WARNINGS!

Many a political leader tried to warn immigrants to the United States that a vote for Lincoln would mean the end of their jobs when all the slaves were set free. Wrote James Gordon Bennett in the *New York Herald*, directing his words to Irish and German workers, "If Lincoln is elected, you will have to compete with the labor of four million emancipated negroes... The North will be flooded with free negroes, and the labor of the white man will be depreciated and degraded."

To be sure, all 15 slave states (see the map of the United States just before the Civil War on page 78) were fearful about the election of Lincoln. Most believed that the United States was a "volunteer" organization of individual states that could separate whenever they chose. And certainly by 1860, most firmly believed that Lincoln's election meant the destruction of the Southern economy and way of life. South Carolina had been the most vocal and unified about secession, so it was perhaps not surprising that it was the first state to carry out the threat.

Indeed, all of the South may have been upset over the election, but in December of 1860, Lincoln wasn't yet in the White House. James Buchanan was. He hadn't done much to settle the slavery issue. What would he do about South Carolina? The answer was pretty much the same—very little, although, in fact, while South Carolina was holding its secession convention in Charleston, Buchanan delivered a speech saying that no state had the right to secede.

The speech was ignored, of course, so Buchanan decided he had better do something else. He asked Congress to come up with yet another compromise, this one to halt further withdrawal from the Union. The response was a proposal from Senator John J. Crittenden of Kentucky.

The Crittenden Compromise would keep slavery in the states where it already existed and in the District of Columbia, would stop interference with interstate slave trade, and would go back to the old dividing line set by the Missouri Compromise of 1820. North of the line, there would be no slavery, ever. South of the line, any new territory would be open to slavery.

But there were no bandages big enough to cover the wounds anymore. Both North and South said no to Crittenden, and the president-elect rejected it anyway. Lincoln stood firm on not expanding slavery into new territory.

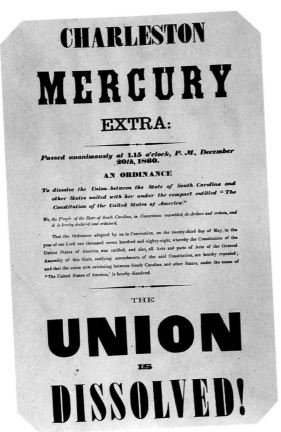

CHARLESTON

MERCURY

EXTRA:

Passed unanimously at 1.15 o'clock, P. M., December 20th, 1860.

AN ORDINANCE

To dissolve the Union between the State of South Carolina and other States united with her under the compact entitled "The Constitution of the United States of America."

We, the People of the State of South Carolina, in Convention assembled, do declare and ordain, and it is hereby declared and ordained,

That the Ordinance adopted by us in Convention, on the twenty-third day of May, in the year of our Lord one thousand seven hundred and eighty-eight, whereby the Constitution of the United States of America, was ratified, and also, all Acts and parts of Acts of the General Assembly of this State, ratifying amendments of the said Constitution, are hereby repealed; and that the union now subsisting between South Carolina and other States, under the name of "The United States of America," is hereby dissolved.

THE

UNION
IS
DISSOLVED!

No turning back. The Charleston Mercury announces the secession of South Carolina on December 20, 1860.

Now Virginia tried to stop the floodgates from opening wider. It called for a peace conference in the nation's capitol. Delegates from 21 states came up with a compromise more or less like Crittenden's. That did not work either. Besides, it was already too late.

Like bowling pins beginning with South Carolina, the slave states began to fall. Mississippi left the Union on January 9, 1861; Florida on January 10; Alabama, January 11; Georgia, January 19; Louisiana, January 26; and Texas, February 1. In Montgomery, Alabama, on February 4, 1861, these seven states declared themselves to be the Confederate States of America. Jefferson Davis of Mississippi was chosen president and a new flag, the Stars and Bars, was designed.

It was surely a sad day for North and South alike. This was the end of all the compromises, all the fights in the halls of Congress, all the accusations and pleadings and calls for common sense and goodwill. The threat was now reality. The strong and vigorous house called the United States of America had divided. It would never be quite the same again.

Perhaps it was unavoidable. Still, some asked why the compromises that had worked so often before could not save the Union once more. But the times were different and so were the leaders. The years had hardened the feelings on both sides of the issues. The great old compromisers such as Daniel Webster and Henry Clay were gone, replaced by Jefferson Davis of Mississippi and Charles Sumner of Massachusetts. These men

FLAGS OF THE CONFEDERACY

The Stars and Bars was the first flag adopted by the Confederacy, but it looked enough like the Stars and Stripes, the U.S. flag, that Rebel troops fired on it by mistake. So, it was replaced with the so-called Battle Flag, which Southern troops most favored. The Stainless Banner became the Confederate national emblem in 1863, but a red band (see the Last Official Flag) was added because the Banner, from a distance, looked too much like a flag of truce.

1. Stars and Bars Flag

2. Battle Flag

3. Stainless Banner Flag

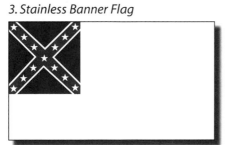

4. Last Official Flag

The flags of the Confederacy are numbered in order of adoption.

were just as patriotic, perhaps, but far less willing to back down on long-held issues.

After secession by the seven Southern states, President Buchanan decided that this was the time to show strength. So, when South Carolina demanded that the U.S. government hand over its property in the South, such as Fort Sumter in Charleston Harbor, Buchanan said no. In fact, he sent supplies to strengthen the fort. However, instead of a naval ship, he dispatched an unarmed merchant vessel, the *Star of the West*. South Carolina wasn't fooled and fired on it. The merchant ship sailed back to New York.

In reality, then, the Civil War began with James Buchanan, not Lincoln, in the White House, for, technically, the United States had been attacked. However, Buchanan seems to have decided to let the newcomer handle it. While he counted the days until he could return to Pennsylvania, the country took a short breather and waited.

Into this mess rode the sixteenth President of the United States, on a train. Actually, he was smuggled into Washington in the dead of night. He arrived on February 23 with a scarf wrapped around his face and quickly checked into the Willard Hotel.

Why all the secrecy? Lincoln had left Illinois on February 11, intending a slow trip east to greet well-wishers. By the time he got to Philadelphia, there were rumors of a murder plot planned for Baltimore. So, the new President started his new life hidden in a crude sleeping berth on a railroad car.

It was not exactly a dignified beginning, but over the next few days Lincoln quietly conducted business from his hotel room. He chose his Cabinet, received visitors, and told the country that his duties were clear, "... marked out by the Constitution."

Finally, it was Inauguration Day, March 4, 1861. It would be hard to imagine a more relieved individual than James Buchanan as he sat beside Lincoln in an open carriage for the drive to the Capitol. Now at last he would be out of the fray. A watchful eye would have noted the hordes of riflemen perched in windows along the way and could not have missed the show of cavalry and infantry protecting the soon-to-be President.

If he was nervous or troubled, the man from Illinois did not show it. Calmly and with dignity, he accepted the office of President of the United States and urged the seceding states to return to the Union. Declaring that no state had a right to secede and that he would not abolish slavery where it already existed, he asked his countrymen to "think calmly and well upon this whole subject." To the South, he said, "You have no oath registered in

Inauguration Day, March 4, 1861. Abraham Lincoln takes the oath of office in a solemn ceremony which will put him in control of the country in its most perilous hour.

A HAPPY MAN, INDEED!

Was James Buchanan glad to be leaving the White House on the morning of March 4, 1861? It would seem so. He said to Lincoln on the way to the inauguration ceremony: "If you are as happy in entering the White House as I shall feel on returning to Wheatland (his home in Pennsylvania), you are a happy man indeed." Unfortunately for the former president, his last years—he died in 1868 at the age of 77—were not as happy as he anticipated. He spent much time defending himself against charges that his nonaction helped to bring about the war. He declared, "I have no regret for any public act of my life, and history will vindicate my memory." That did not happen.

Heaven to destroy the Government, while I shall have the most solemn one to 'preserve, protect and defend it.'" Then, passionately he appealed to the South. "We are not enemies but friends," he declared. "We must not be enemies. Though passion may have strained, it must not break our bonds of affection." And again, "In your hands, my dissatisfied fellow countrymen, and not in mine, is the momentous issue of civil war. The government will not assail you. You can have no conflict, without being yourselves the aggressors...."

But, of course, it was too late. The eloquence fell on deaf ears. The South had seceded, and there was no turning back. The Union was broken. The house was divided.

Secession: No Turning Back

Jefferson Davis, former U.S. senator from Mississippi, was pruning his rosebushes on the afternoon of February 10, 1861. The 53-year-old Davis was a tall, gaunt man with a twitching cheek. This nervous tic would eventually lead to blindness in one eye. Davis was so formal and standoffish that he disliked calling people by their first names, even slaves. He did, however, enjoy the calm and quiet of Brierfield, his plantation near Vicksburg. But on this particular afternoon, any calmness in his life was shattered forever as a slave rushed across the lawn and handed him a printed message.

The former Varina Howell was a young woman from Natchez, Davis's second wife and 18 years his junior. She later said that her dignified husband read the message and looked as though he had just been given a death sentence. As in a sense, he had. For in this manner, Jefferson Davis learned that he had been elected president of the Provisional Government of the Confederate States of America.

The government that Davis was to head was formally only two days old by the time the news reached him. On February 8, the delegates from the seven seceding states had adopted a

A dedicated man but formal and aloof to the extreme, Jefferson Davis surely had mixed feelings when he learned he was now the president of the Confederate States of America.

constitution. Although it differed little from the U.S. Constitution, it declared each state to be independent, implying that it could secede at any time. The president and vice president would serve only one six-year term.

Davis was not the first or unanimous choice. Quiet, gloomy, often stubborn and distant, he was a hard man to get to know. Sam Houston said he was "cold as a lizard." But the new nation didn't have time to search for a leader or hold an election. It needed a president right now, and Davis looked like the best available choice. He was not too conservative nor too radical. His honesty and loyalty to duty and to the South were above reproach. He would present a dignified front to the angry North.

Davis accepted, of course, but he really didn't want the job. He had hoped to be given command of the Southern armies. On paper, Davis seemed like an excellent military man. He had graduated from West Point (1828) and was secretary of war in the Cabinet of Franklin Pierce (1853-57). His own father, Samuel Emory Davis, was a veteran of the American Revolution. But, in fact, Davis's military judgment was often poor, and he rarely accepted advice from his commanders. An unemotional man, he inspired little devotion from those under him and even less from his vice president, Alexander H. Stephens of Georgia. Stephens, who really couldn't stand Davis, was gloomy about secession anyway. He was convinced from the start that the South could never win and spent most of the war at home.

Jefferson, born in Georgia, was the tenth and last child in the Davis family. They moved to Mississippi when he was three years old. After his military schooling, Davis fought in the Black Hawk War under future president Zachary Taylor. In 1835, when Davis was said to have been "handsome and witty," he married Taylor's daughter, Sarah. The young couple settled near Vicksburg, Mississippi, where, within three months, Sarah contracted a fever

IF I CAN'T BE PRESIDENT, I'M NOT GOING TO PLAY!

Not everyone was pleased with the choice of Jefferson Davis for president of the Confederate States of America. Certainly not Robert A. Toombs (1810-85) of Georgia. After Lincoln's election, Toombs, then in the U.S. Senate, began to call for secession. He resigned from the Senate and was a delegate to the convention in Montgomery that established the Confederacy. The choice for president narrowed to two strong contenders— Jefferson Davis and Toombs—with the delegates rather equally divided. Then Toombs made a fatal mistake. He attended a dinner party two days before the convention was to vote. Supposedly, Toombs emerged from the party "falling-down drunk." Jefferson became president and Toombs went off by himself to sulk.

In an effort to restore harmony, Davis offered Toombs the top Cabinet job of secretary of state. Toombs accepted, but not with good grace. He continually criticized Davis and finally left the government after a few months. He was wounded in the battle for Antietam and when a promotion did not come, he left the army too.

and died. A grief-sticken Davis stayed almost alone for seven years, working on his plantation and studying constitutional law.

Ten years after Sarah's death, Davis married Varina Howell and was elected to the U.S. Congress. He resigned to fight in the war with Mexico, was severely wounded, and returned home a hero after fighting at the Battle of Buena Vista. After election to the Senate, Franklin Pierce chose him to be secretary of war.

A dedicated Southerner, Davis nevertheless opposed secession when South Carolina withdrew from the Union. He did, however, believe that Lincoln's election would prove disastrous to the South. After Mississippi seceded in January 1861, Davis, in his farewell Senate speech, pleaded for peace and then went home to Brierfield, where the Confederacy found him.

With heavy heart but firm resolve, Jefferson Davis left for Montgomery, Alabama. On the steps of the state capitol, February 18, 1861, he was sworn in as the first—and as it turned out, only—president of the Confederate States of America. After his speech, the crowd broke out in a spirited version of a popular minstrel tune called "Dixie." "I wish I was in the land of cotton" can still strike feelings of loyalty or disdain today, depending upon what side of the Mason-Dixon line you stand on. The boundary between Pennsylvania and Maryland, surveyed in 1763-67 by Englishmen Charles Mason and Jeremiah Dixon, became the separation line between free and slave states. It is still sometimes used today when distinguishing between North and South.

By nature, Davis was not an optimistic man and he saw nothing in this swearing-in ceremony to cheer him. Davis wrote to his wife: "The audience was large and brilliant. Upon my weary heart was showered smiles, plaudits, and flowers, but beyond them, I saw trouble and thorns innumerable." He also could have said that the brand new Confederacy was, to put it mildly, in chaos. Everything was topsy-turvy. Davis and his quickly-put-together government met in a hotel room; the secretary of the treasury had to buy his own desk and chair in order to work; when asked where his department was located, Robert Toombs, new Confederate secretary of state, said, "In my hat." The first Confederate money was printed by a New York firm because there was no suitable printing press in the South.

For all his devotion to duty, Jefferson Davis was a realist. Far more so than the majority of his fellow countrymen. Most Southerners believed that secession would not bring on war. And if it did, how could the much smaller Confederacy hope to stand up to the much larger Union? The South had the answer to that, too. Cotton. The South grew cotton, which was one of the reasons it

depended so on slave labor. The world needed cotton. In fact, at the time of the Civil War the demand for cotton worldwide was extremely high. This demand, reasoned the South, would bring high prices. And high prices would entice such countries as Mexico, Cuba, and parts of Central America to join a Southern confederation. The South in general could see only good things from secession—no more arguments over slavery, no high tariffs to pay on manufactured goods from the North, no insults from preachy Northerners over that "peculiar institution."

The scene looks calm as Jefferson Davis takes office, but few, including the new Confederate leader himself, are confident of victory.

"DIXIE" AND "YANKEE DOODLE"

Troops on both sides of the Civil War went into battle singing. The popular Southern minstrel tune was rewritten by Dan Emmett, a Northerner, and became "Dixie."

I wish I was in the land of cotton
Old times there are not forgotten
Look away, look away, look away, Dixie land.

Southern troops often sang "Yankee Doodle" as an insult to the Union. No one knows exactly how and where the name "yankee" orginated, but it is thought to have been in common use in 1683 by pirates of the Spanish Main to refer to Dutchmen.

Father and I went down to camp
Along with Captain Gooden
And there we saw the men and boys
As thick as hasty puddin'

Or: Yankee Doodle went up town
Upon a little pony
He stuck a feather in his cap
And called it macaroni

Soldiers of the North had many inspiring songs of their own to send them into battle, including "The Battle Hymn of the Republic," by Julia Ward Howe.

Of course, things didn't exactly work out that way. One of the strangest things about the Civil War is that until the first guns were fired, neither side really understood that the other actually meant to fight. The North had been hearing secession talk for so long that it had become just another game of politics. You threatened, but you didn't really do anything. And the average Southerner reasoned that if Northerners hated the South and slavery so much, wouldn't they be glad to get rid of both? Why fight?

The South also felt it had something else going for it—a fiercely passionate devotion to a culture and a way of life. Any Johnny Reb, a nickname for Southern troops often used by the Union soldiers, was willing to die for the Southland. How could the "flood of immigrants and money-mad Yankees" in the North stand up to that?

These independent people lived in the 11 slave states that would become the Confederate States of America. Seven of the 11 seceded before Fort Sumter, and four after. But whenever they left the Union and whatever their specific circumstances, they were totally united in their fierce dedication to the cause. For that reason alone, they would sometimes be successful in battle against overwhelming odds.

One of the original 13 colonies, settled by the English in 1670, South Carolina was the first state to secede—December 20, 1860. Cotton had become an important plantation crop in the state after 1800. When the free black Denmark Vesey planned a revolt in Charleston in 1822, South Carolinians grew agitated over the touchy subject of slavery, even though the plot was discovered and Vesey hanged. And when high tariffs were set by the federal government in 1828, there was early talk of disunion. In fact, South Carolina called for a convention to do away with the tax laws in 1832, loudly supported by its senator, John C. Calhoun. Vice president under Jackson, Calhoun had resigned in 1832 and become a U.S. senator. He was a "spokesman for the South" even as vice president, however. But the rest of the South would not go along with Calhoun's request.

Other South Carolina radicals led the march to secession. They met in Charleston for a convention on December 17, 1860. The entire state government was on hand as well as other wealthy Southerners. The subject was getting out of the Union and tempers were hot. It took three days to get to the point, but at 1:15 p.m. on December 20, 1860, all 169 delegates adopted the following ordinance:

> We, the people of the State of South Carolina, in Convention assembled, do declare and ordain...that the union now subsisting between South Carolina and other states under the name of "The United States of America" is hereby dissolved.

Mississippi was quick to follow. It called for a convention, and on January 9, 1861, the vote was 84 to 15 to leave the Union. This

THE UNITED STATES JUST BEFORE THE CIVIL WAR

Slavery was the great dividing issue of the American Civil War. There were other differences, too, but on the lighter side, and not serious enough to fight over. For example, the contrast between the Northerners' busy city life and the slow and easy plantation style in the South: A Mississippian commented, "The Northerner loves to make money, the Southerner to spend it."

By the start of the Civil War, New York City boasted a population of nearly one million and Chicago more than 100,000. Cities such as Boston and Philadelphia were growing at a great rate. With the exception of New Orleans, Southern cities were relatively small. Charleston, Savannah, and Richmond each had fewer than 40,000 people. A visiting Yankee said that from the look of Southern towns, "the stranger would think that business was taking a siesta."

The Confederate States of America face the United States of America at the start of the Civil War. Note that with the exception of California and Oregon, most of the midwestern and western lands are not yet organized into states

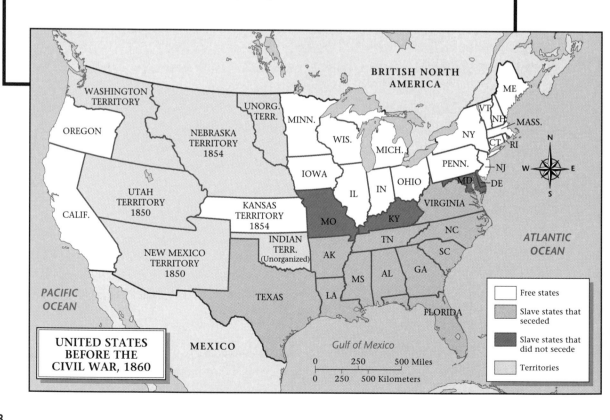

UNITED STATES BEFORE THE CIVIL WAR, 1860

Legend:
- Free states
- Slave states that seceded
- Slave states that did not secede
- Territories

was no surprise, of course, for Mississippi's economy was greatly tied to cotton with its huge plantations and slave population. Strangely, however, owning slaves was not a common practice among Mississippi's small landowners, who far outnumbered the larger planters. Yet, the small farmer had little say in political affairs at the time. These differences led to much division within the state on the issue of slavery.

A day after the Mississippi vote, on January 10, Florida joined the Confederacy. First settled by the Spanish, Florida began to develop economically only after 1821 when the United States took possession. By the time of the Civil War, a small farm and plantation economy was thriving. Although it quickly joined the Confederacy, Florida would not be much involved in the war.

Close on the heels of Florida came Alabama, which then joined the Confederacy on January 11, 1861. By the midnineteenth century, Alabama was a land where cotton was king and nearly half of the residents were black, a large percentage of them slaves. From the start, Alabama was deeply involved in the steps that led to war. The first Confederate capital was established at Montgomery, the state capital, and the legislature raised money for military operations and to help support military families.

Georgia followed its neighbors into the Confederacy on January 19. By the time of the Civil War, Georgia, having the greatest number of true

RHETT THE FIRE-EATER

No one was happier over the decision to secede than Robert Barnwell Rhett, the fire-eating editor of the Charleston *Mercury*.

He declared the firing on Sumter to be the "opening bell of the Revolution." Far from being apologetic, Rhett proclaimed South Carolina "honored to be the first thus to resist the Yankee tyranny.... She has not hesitated to strike the first blow, full in the face of her insulter." Said Rhett, "We would not exchange or recall that blow for millions! It has wiped out a half century of scorn and outrage."

Always a larger-than-life figure, Sam Houston, former frontier hero, represented Texas in the U.S. Senate 1846–59.

plantations in the South, had come to view slavery as totally necessary to its economic survival. Therefore, slave owner or not, most white Georgians were all for secession.

Louisiana took a little more than a month to follow South Carolina's lead. It left the Union on January 26, 1861. That is perhaps a little surprising for even though a convention voted to secede, the people seemed to be rather evenly divided. The division rested largely with the state's economy—the wealthy plantation owners, who needed slavery, and the small farmers, who felt that their economic future rested with the Union.

Texas joined the Confederate States of America on February 1. This largest state in the Union at the time had long been the scene of battle between American settlers and Mexicans. In 1836, Texas became an independent republic for a strife-filled ten years, with Sam Houston as president, and did not become the twenty-eighth state until 1845. Even in joining the Confederacy, there was turmoil. Governor Sam Houston was strongly pro-Union and refused to take an oath of allegiance to the Confederacy even after secession. Consequently, he was thrown out of office.

After the firing on Fort Sumter on April 12, 1861, and President Lincoln's demand for soldiers to fight the rebels, four Southern states seceded to bring the total in the Confederacy to 11. Virginia was the first of the four, seceding on April 17.

Loyal to the South but hoping to avoid bloodshed, Virginia had not joined the original seven. It could not, however, do battle against its Southern neighbors. Although Virginia had abolished the African slave trade in 1778, it still had more slaves than any other state. Thirty years before the Civil War (in 1831), a bloody uprising led by the slave Nat Turner had raised great tension on the issue of slavery in the state.

Once Virginia seceded, the Confederate capital was moved from Montgomery, Alabama, to Richmond. The state was the scene of many battles and much destruction during the Civil War. Even before the war's end, it had lost one-third of its territory as West Virginia separated from Virginia in 1861, carved out of Virginia's western portion, and was declared a state of the Union in 1863.

Arkansas followed Virginia on May 6. Despite being a slave state, Union sentiment was very strong in northern Arkansas, and about 6,000 white soldiers fought for the Union, compared to some 58,000 for the South.

Virginia's border state to the south, North Carolina, left the Union on May 20. Although closely tied to South Carolina— the boundaries between the two had not been completely surveyed until 1821, North Carolina, in contrast, joined the Confederacy with reluctance. It had favored and fought for compromise. But once committed, North Carolinians threw themselves into the fight for independence, although some remained loyal to the United States.

Tennessee, the last state to join the Confederacy, on June 8, was loyal to the Union right up until Lincoln called for volunteers. Only Virginia saw more fighting during the Civil War. Battles at Shiloh, Chattanooga, Knoxville, and Nashville were scenes of great tragedy and loss. Many people in Tennessee, however, did not support the Confederacy and remained loyal to the Union. In fact, Andrew Johnson, who would later be Lincoln's second vice president, was the only Southern senator who did not leave the Senate when his state seceded.

As He Saw It

Jefferson Davis may have voiced a moderate tone in his acceptance speech, but Vice President Alexander H. Stephens did not fear the anger of the opposition. "Our new government is founded on the opposite idea of the equality of the races," he declared. "Its corner stone rests upon the great truth that the Negro is not equal to the white man. This... government is the first in the history of the world, based upon this great physical and moral truth."

The extreme views of such Southern leaders as Alexander H. Stephens broadened the gap between North and South.

Perhaps the true tragedy of the Civil War is that both sides would learn all too soon and far too late how wrong they were to think that the other side would not fight. Even Jefferson Davis, when accepting the presidency, sent a message of moderation to President Lincoln. In his acceptance speech, Davis said that the South just wanted to be left alone, although it would defend itself if attacked. Even some Northerners began to feel that perhaps the best thing would be to "let the erring sisters go in peace."

But for Lincoln, this was difficult to do. By the time he took office, the Confederates had seized all federal forts and navy yards in the seceding states, with two exceptions, Fort Pickens, off the Florida coast at Pensacola and Fort Sumter in Charleston Harbor, South Carolina. Davis's first official act as president of the Confederacy was to send a peace commission to Washington. Lincoln, who did not acknowledge the Confederacy's right to secede, refused to see its members. For his part, Lincoln seemed to be doing very little about the situation. In his inaugural speech, he had vowed that he would "hold, occupy, and possess" all federal property. The next day, however, he received word from Major Robert Anderson, in command of Fort Sumter, that in the face of South Carolina's threat to take the fort, it could be

held only if men and food supplies were sent immediately. Lincoln did nothing. Government leaders began to wonder if they had another Buchanan on their hands. By the time he did act, most of his Cabinet members were convinced they could run the government far better than he. Besieged by differing opinions, the new President was merely listening to all sides and then making up his own mind.

Most of Lincoln's Cabinet did not want him to send supplies to Fort Sumter, fearing that would provoke war. But the President had vowed to protect federal property. He was determined not to lose either Fort Pickens or Fort Sumter to the Confederates. Knowing that armed ships would be taken as a sign of attack, he decided to send unarmed vessels carrying only

As determined for the cause as any Southerner, thousands of New Yorkers gather in Union Square to demand victory as a damaged U.S. flag carried from Fort Sumter waves atop a statue of George Washington, April 20, 1861.

food to both forts. As he wrote to Francis W. Pickens, governor of South Carolina, "If such attempt be not resisted, no effort to throw in men, arms, or ammunition will be made without further notice, or in case of an attack upon the Fort." The governor sent the message on to Jefferson Davis in Montgomery.

Lincoln had, of course, thrown the ball into the Confederate court. By April 6, his message had arrived in Montgomery. Davis called his Cabinet together, upset that Lincoln had done exactly what he promised in his inaugural speech. He had squeezed the South into a position where it might very well have to fire the first shot. But Davis didn't want to do that anymore than Lincoln did.

The arguments went back and forth. There seemed no way to back out. The people of the Confederacy demanded war. If Davis didn't act, South Carolina might very well do so on its own. In the end, everyone in the Cabinet but Secretary of State Toombs favored an attack. Warned Toombs, "... firing upon that fort will inaugurate a civil war greater than any the world has yet seen."

And so, on April 10, the leader of the Confederate forces in Charleston received a telegraph from Secretary of War Leroy Pope Walker in Montgomery, Alabama. Demand Sumter's evacuation, it said. If Anderson refused, "proceed… as you may determine...."

That night, hysteria seemed to take over the city of Charleston. Bonfires sprang up everywhere and drums rolled through the dark hours. Parades snaked through the streets as the people of the South prepared themselves for the "glorious adventure."

War Begins:
Firing on Fort Sumter

6

The people of Charleston, South Carolina, woke to warm temperatures and cloudy skies on this last day of peace, April 11, 1861. The weather was noted by Mary Chesnut, wife of James, a colonel on the staff of Pierre G.T. Beauregard, the dapper brigadier general from Louisiana who commanded the Confederate forces in the city. Or, perhaps Mrs. Chesnut was commenting on the possibility of war when she wrote in her diary that evening: "And so we fool on, into the black cloud ahead of us."

IT PAYS TO KEEP A DIARY!

But for the fact that Mary Chesnut decided to keep a diary, she might never have found her way into the history books. Although her husband was in the army, she had no official standing or duties, except to act as hostess during dinner parties. But Mary, a good friend of Confederate president Jefferson Davis and his wife, was a keen observer of events. She began her diary in early 1861 as history began to swirl about her. A moody woman and often depressed, she tried to collect her thoughts into her journal entries. But Mary Chesnut found little to bring her tranquillity that spring. About slavery she said, "God forgive us but ours is a monstrous system." On the Civil War, "This Southern Confederacy must be supported now by calm determination and cool brains. We have risked all and we must play our best, for the stake is life or death."

As he posed for a photograph, little did Major Robert Anderson know that his duty assignment to Fort Sumter would give him a prominent spot in history books.

By noon that day, if not a black cloud, certainly an ominous one settled over the Chesnut household. James was given orders by General Beauregard to row out to Fort Sumter, the tiny Federal post about three miles out in Charleston Harbor. There, he delivered a handwritten message to Major Robert Anderson, the fort commander. After reading the demand for surrender, Anderson wrote a polite reply, saying in effect, no thank you. Then, still in friendly fashion, he walked Chesnut out to the wharf to see him off. In parting, Anderson asked the colonel if Beauregard would be likely to fire on the fort without further warning. Chesnut didn't think so. Anderson nodded and declared that, fire or not, the Federal troops would be starved out in a few days anyway.

Was Major Anderson suggesting he would surrender? General Beauregard thought perhaps so. Back on shore, he relayed that thought to Confederate Secretary of War Walker. Hoping to get the fort without firing a shot, Walker sent Chesnut rowing back with another message. In essence, it said: "Tell us when you'll leave and we won't shoot."

This time, Anderson took three hours to talk it over with his officers. By now, it was three o'clock on the morning of April 12. Anderson finally told Chesnut that the Federal troops would surrender in three days, unless they had orders from Washington to the contrary, or unless they got supplies, or unless...

Chesnut figured Anderson was stalling and said so.

Still polite, however, he wrote a formal declaration to the Federal commander. It stated: "We have the honor to notify you... we will open fire... in one hour."

Why was South Carolina, and thereby the entire Confederacy, so intent about getting Fort Sumter? It was just a tiny place guarded by less than 100 Federal troops. What did it matter? As it turned out, a lot. The flag of the United States of America waving over the fort was an offense to the seceding states. How could an independent nation, as the Confederacy proclaimed itself to be, put up with a foreign fort right in the middle of one of its principal harbors? But President Lincoln had said he was duty bound to hold on to all Federal property and by that he certainly meant the five-sided brick stronghold in the waters of Charleston Harbor.

Besides, even though both sides were not in the least ready for war nor had the slightest idea of the toll it would take in human lives and suffering, both North and South almost seemed to welcome it. The squabbling and bitterness and false alarms had been going on for so long that doing anything was a relief.

It was four in the morning by the time Chesnut got back to the mainland to deliver the latest news. Beauregard ordered the guns to fire at 4:30. The honor of the first shot went to a civilian, Congressman Roger Pryor of Virginia. But when he realized he would go down in history as the man who started the war, he declined. However, what with a number of cannon going off at the same time anyway, it is probably impossible to say who fired the first shot. But among the first was elderly Edmund Ruffin, also of Virginia, who had long called for secession. Ruffin's place in history did not bother him in the least. He later said he was delighted to perform the service.

By whatever hand, the first shots slammed into Fort Sumter at 4:30 a.m., April 12, 1861. The Civil War had begun. For the first few moments, some of the Federal troops stood awestruck as they watched the high fiery arc of the shells. A few comments were made on the poor aim of the Confederates. Sanity returned quickly, however, as they all suddenly seemed to realize where they were standing and hurried inside. Oddly enough, no one was killed during this first battle of a war that, directly or indirectly, took the lives of more than 600,000 Americans.

In an act of futile defiance, Fort Sumter withstood 34 hours of bombardment from batteries on shore.

Some months before, Major Anderson had been sent to command Fort Sumter by President Buchanan's secretary of war, John B. Floyd, who was decidedly pro-Confederacy. Floyd thought Anderson to be the likely man in an explosive situation. Translation: Floyd believed that Anderson—Kentucky-born, married to a Georgia woman, and a former slave owner—would certainly favor the South if a choice had to be made. What Floyd hadn't counted on was Major Anderson's unswerving sense of duty.

Anderson may have been new to his post, but he certainly understood the danger he was in. He was well aware that the new President had vowed to hold on to Federal territory—that meant Anderson and his men. But how could they defend this place? Anderson had sent a letter to Lincoln, which arrived on March 5, 1861. The new President had been in office for all of one day. What the message said, more or less, was that about 20,000 troops were needed to hold the fort and harbor, that their food and other supplies were dwindling, and—this was only a hint—that perhaps it might be a good idea to withdraw.

Lincoln talked with his Cabinet about defending and reinforcing Fort Sumter. No one was very enthusiastic. In fact, Winfield Scott, Lincoln's general in charge of the army, said that, in light of the fact that war seemed imminent, the fort couldn't be reinforced in time anyway.

In this air of pessimism, Lincoln sent Gustavus V. Fox, a retired naval officer, down to Charleston. Fox asked the Confederates if he could row out to see Anderson. They agreed but wouldn't let him go alone. Since Fox couldn't talk to Anderson in private, he could only hint that reinforcements were being planned in Washington.

The workings of government sometimes move slowly. It was not until April 4 that Anderson got word—and not even by special courier!—that relief supplies were coming. No date was given. And the President made clear to Anderson that he was being sent supplies only, no military weapons. Lincoln did not want to provoke South Carolina into war.

Lincoln also sent a message to South Carolina's governor, Francis Pickens. It said that the relief mission was strictly peaceful. Pickens relayed the message to the Charleston commander, General Beauregard. The general may have had the reputation of being too concerned with his appearance, but Beauregard was, like Anderson, equally concerned with duty. Since early April, he had been bringing in reinforcements. In addition to cannon, howitzers, and mortars, Beauregard now had about 6,000 men against Anderson's 68. Of course, some of them were not exactly battle tested. Augustus Dickert, for instance, was 15 years old and had been in a sweat to get to Charleston since he heard the news that the fort might be attacked. Dickert was terrified that the fight would be over before he got into it.

The Civil War was two hours old by the time Anderson and his men fired back. They had assembled at 6 a.m. and had breakfast. Being soldiers, they grumbled about the food, but this time they had reason, for without supplies, there was nothing left to eat but salt pork.

Anderson had more problems at the moment than the food supply. How was he going to fight back? How was he going to defend the fort? His biggest guns, 26 of them, were the only ones that could really do some damage. But they were up on the top level of Fort Sumter, called the barbette tier, and right out in the open. If he sent his men up there, they could easily be picked off.

Anderson decided to fire the 21 guns on the lower level. These cannon were quite effective against oncoming ships. Of course, there were no oncoming ships, only the Confederates hidden behind earthen walls on the shore. But the smaller guns would have to do until help arrived.

The honor of the first shot against the Confederates in the Civil War went to Captain Abner Doubleday. Although he would rise to the rank of general, Doubleday's first shot of the war was not so heroic. He missed the target. The shell sailed right over the iron battery that protected the Confederates.

EXTREME ODDS: ONE SOLDIER FIGHTS THE CONFEDERACY

Major Anderson told his men that it was too dangerous to fire the cannons on Sumter's barbette tier. But Sergeant John Carmody couldn't resist. Against orders, of course, he quietly made his way to the top of the fort. The big guns were aimed right at Fort Moultrie across the harbor, so he fired them, one after another. For just a few minutes, it was John Carmody, U.S. Army, versus the Confederate States of America! Presumably, Anderson couldn't help but hear the forbidden guns, but at the moment he had more on his mind than yelling at Sergeant Carmody.

DOUBLEDAY STRIKES OUT!

The name of Abner Doubleday (1819-93), of Ballston Spa, New York, is linked to the U.S. national pasttime—baseball. Supposedly, he was the original inventor of the game, although that story is doubted by many sports historians. Doubleday attended school in Cooperstown, New York, before going on to West Point, graduating in 1842. He fought in the Seminole War in Florida (1856-58) and commanded the gunners at Fort Sumter. After Sumter, Doubleday fought at the second battle of Bull Run, at Antietam, Fredericksburg, and Gettysburg, eventually reaching the temporary rank of major general. He retired from the army in 1873.

In 1907, a commission headed by Albert G. Spalding decided that in 1839, at Cooperstown, New York, Doubleday had devised the original rules of the game of baseball. Accordingly, in 1936, Cooperstown was designated as the home of the Baseball Hall of Fame and Museum, which honors the best players of the game.

The Federal troops returned fire bravely but with little success against the Confederates. Hours passed and the bombardment continued. The fort itself held up rather well at first. After all, almost nothing could penetrate the thick outer walls. Almost more of a danger than the exploding shells was the constant threat of fire. The outer walls of the barracks were wood covered with brick. The Confederates used an old trick to get around that. They heated some of the cannon balls in an oven before firing. The red hot shells stuck in the walls and set the wood on fire.

Whether deserving or not, Abner Doubleday is forever linked to the game of baseball, shown here in its infancy.

The shells kept coming in, the Federals kept firing back, and the fires kept breaking out. Where were the supply ships? Finally, a cheer went up from the fort in early afternoon. A ship had been sighted! Help was near. Anderson lowered and raised the flag to let the supply ship know they still held the fort.

It was indeed the supply ship. Gustavus Fox was aboard the *Baltic* where he had been waiting for some time for another seven ships to appear. By six o'clock that evening, only the cutter *Harriet Lane* and the sloop *Pawnee* had joined the supply force. Fox decided to go in, along with the *Harriet Lane*. But when he got a little closer to the fort and realized it was under heavy fire, he sailed out again. It was decided to wait until nightfall and row in the supplies.

Both sides slowed down for the night, helped by a rainstorm that put out some of the fires. Anderson sent his men on an inspection of the fort. The general opinion was that Sumter was a ruined mess, but it would fight on.

The attack was renewed with great force the following morning, April 13. Soon, wherever there was wood in the fort, it was burning. Worse yet, Anderson realized that several hundred barrels of powder were in real danger of exploding. Someone had unwisely stored them right next to a wooden structure. Anderson ordered the barrels to be rolled to safety, a most dangerous task. At any moment, they could blow up. Amazingly, they did not.

While the troops in the fort could scarcely breathe in the smoky air, Fox was having his troubles at sea. Choppy waters made it impossible to load supplies. Almost all the Union guns were silent now, but the Confederate bombardment increased. The South knew the fort was about to fall. But in tribute to the bravery of the Union troops, the Confederates cheered anytime a shot rang out from the fort.

For 34 long hours, Anderson and his men stood the attack under impossible odds. The Confederates fired more than 3,000 shells at the ruined fort. Either through sheer luck or incredibly bad marksmanship, only eight men, four on each side, were injured, not from the shelling but from flying brick and other broken framents.

When the end finally came, it was, to say the least, confusing. A shell hit the fort's flagstaff and knocked it over. General Beauregard figured that Anderson was surrendering at last. He sent out three aides in a boat. Unbeknownst to him, however, Senator Louis Wigfall of Texas, who had been watching the bombardment from a safe distance, decided it was time to become a hero. In a small boat with one private and two slaves, he sailed out to the fort waving a white handkerchief.

In all the smoke, no one saw him coming. The Union troops were quite surprised when Wigfall suddenly appeared waving his handkerchief. He politely asked to see Major Anderson. While a soldier ran off to get him, Wigfall kept on waving. Anderson appeared and, thinking Wigfall was Beauregard's legitimate envoy, agreed to surrender. He had little choice. His supplies were nearly gone and his men exhausted.

So the Stars and Stripes was taken down and a white flag hoisted. Wigfall was tremendously pleased with himself and rowed back to shore.

However, this cloth waving and flag hoisting confused those

The Confederate flag flies above Fort Sumter. The Union has been defeated in the first battle of the Civil War.

on shore and especially the three aides who were still rowing out
to the fort to ask for Anderson's surrender. When they delivered
Beauregard's request, Anderson was not only confused himself
but angry as well.

What about Wigfall? Beauregard's aides had to admit that the
senator shouldn't have been there at all. Now Anderson really
became angry and told them to forget the whole thing. The battle
was on again.

The aides apologized and urged Anderson to think it over. He
did. By this time, Beauregard had sent another group of aides
rowing out to the fort to find out what was going on. Cool heads
finally prevailed and a surrender agreement was reached that
evening. The battle for Fort Sumter, the first of the Civil War,
was over.

The terms were honorable. The Federal troops would remain
in what was left of the fort until the morning of April 14.
Anderson was given permission to fire a 100-gun salute to the
tattered U.S. flag. With tears in his eyes, the U.S. commander
thanked his former student, Beauregard, for allowing the salute.
With good grace, the dapper Southern general stated that he
would allow the Federal troops to depart the fort before his own
men took it over.

However, when 50 shots of the Federal salute had been fired,
there was an accident. It killed Private Daniel Hough. When
another accident killed a second soldier, Anderson ordered the
salute stopped.

Carrying the torn flag, Major Anderson marched quietly from
the fort, followed by his men. Ironically, he would return to
Sumter and raise that same flag four years later, this time as a
general. The following day, the Northern troops boarded the still
waiting *Baltic* for the sail home.

The news of Sumter's fall greeted a saddened President

Lincoln, but there was great rejoicing in the South. The Confederate flag was hoisted over a nearly destroyed fort after what seemed an incredibly easy victory. The war had begun with a Southern triumph. Proclaimed the headlines of the Charleston *Mercury*: The Battle of Fort Sumter! End of the Fight! Major Anderson Surrenders!

President Lincoln acted quickly. He called for an immediate blockade of all Southern ports. On April 15, 1861, he sent out a call for troops to all states in the Union. When Sumter fell, the North had an army of barely 16,000 men. Lincoln called for 75,000. Throughout the United States, men rushed to answer the call to arms.

But the call left some with a terrible decision to make. Eight slave states were still in the Union. In four of them—Arkansas, North Carolina, Tennessee, and Virginia —not everyone was totally

With the first battle of the war lost to the Confederacy, the North erupted in patriotism. Here, a recruiting wagon tours Philadelphia seeking army volunteers. It was not necessary to draft men into military service until two years after the war began.

sympathetic to the Southern cause. They had not yet seceded because they hoped that bloodshed could be avoided. But once they were called on to provide troops against their Southern neighbors, they withdrew. Now, Jefferson Davis began arrangements to transfer his government capital from Montgomery to Richmond, Virginia.

But what about the remaining four—the so-called border states of Delaware, Kentucky, Maryland, Missouri—as well as the mountainous western section of Virginia, which disagreed with

PATRIOTS – NORTH AND SOUTH

The firing on Fort Sumter produced some quick and usually patriotic reactions in the American public. Here are parts of some letters written following the start of war.

James Jackson of Alabama wrote to his brother, "They are volunteering right smartly here. If you want to join a company, come down here and let's go together. I have a notion of trying it a while."

Centenary College in Louisiana got right to the point with this terse notice: "Students have all gone to war. College suspended."

Private Ted Upson of Indiana showed a romantic streak: "We was treated as good as company could be at every station... We got kisses from the girls at a good many places and we returned the same to them."

Private Peter Wilson of Iowa was a little more practical. He wrote, "I have got the best suit of clothes that I ever had in my life."

And to William Nugent of Mississippi, the war presented an unpleasant choice, as it would to many: "I feel that I would like to shoot a Yankee, and yet I know this would not be in harmony with the spirit of Christianity."

They came from all over the country to fight, at least one known to be only nine years old.

Right: Volunteers of the 1st Virginia Military - the Richmond Grays.

Below: A Union officer is bid farewell by a loved one who kisses his sword.

the aims of the South and wanted to separate from the state? Lincoln was desperate to keep these border areas in the Union. What would they do?

Of all the border states, Delaware was the most likely to remain. First settled in 1631, it still had slaves at the start of the Civil War, but the number was down to 1,800. Named for Baron De La Warr, a governor of Virginia, Delaware was very proud of the fact that its speedy ratification of the Constitution, December 7, 1787, had earned it the right to call itself the "first state." More importantly, it was economically tied to the Northern states. Although it never voted for Lincoln, pro-Union it would remain.

Kentucky, the fifteenth state in the Union, stayed neutral for several months. At the start of the war, those who favored slavery had control of the government and Kentucky's governor was pro-Confederate. There were, however, only a few large slaveholders by that time, and about one-quarter of the state's population was black. Eventually, the state stayed with the Union, and during the war about 90,000 Kentucky soldiers fought for the North and about 40,000 for the South.

Maryland had trouble making up its mind. One of the original 13 states on the Atlantic seaboard, Maryland's people were very divided. The wealthy and land-owning upper classes sided with the South. The working population, tied to economic interests in the North, wanted to remain with the Union. A third group called for the state to stay neutral. Finally, Maryland agreed to remain with the Union. However, 20,000 Maryland men joined the Confederate army, and 46,000 fought for the North.

Missouri was pro-Union with a governor who wanted to secede. It had become a slave state after the passage of the Missouri Compromise in 1820. In the end though, divided in its sympathy and sentiment, Missouri stayed with the Union. About a quarter of

A Union regiment marches down a main street in Providence, Rhode Island, early in the war.

men in the state, however, eventually joined the Confederate army.

When the Civil War started, the western section of Virginia renewed its cries for separation. West Virginia became the thirty-fifth state in the Union in 1863.

The sides were clearly drawn. In his inaugural speech, Abraham Lincoln had implored his countrymen to remain friends. In this April of 1861, they were friends no more. The United States and the Confederacy, Yankee and Rebel, Blue and Gray had become mortal enemies. It was too late to save a country now aflame with anger and hatred and a house now divided.

Chronology of Important Events

1619   First Africans brought to the Colonies, at Jamestown, VA, as indentured servants.

1787   Constitutional Convention meets.

1803   United States gets Louisiana Purchase from France.

1808   Congress bans African slave trade.

1809   Abraham Lincoln born, February 12.

1812   Louisiana becomes 18th state; rest of Purchase organized into Missouri Territory.

1816   Indiana becomes 19th state.

1817   Mississippi becomes 20th state; American Colonization Society formed.

1818   Illinois becomes 21st state.

1819   Tallmadge Resolution over Missouri Territory defeated in Congress, February 13; Alabama becomes 22nd state, bringing Union total to 11 free states, 11 slave states.

1820   Missouri Compromise; Maine becomes 23rd state.

1821   Missouri becomes 24th state.

1822   Denmark Vesey plans slave uprising, Charleston, SC.

1831   Nat Turner slave uprising; William Lloyd Garrison starts *The Liberator* and American Anti-Slavery Society.

1836   Arkansas becomes 25th state.

1837   Michigan becomes 26th state.

1845   Florida becomes 27th state; Texas becomes 28th state.

1846   War with Mexico (1846-48); Wilmot Proviso, banning slavery in territory taken from Mexico in war; Iowa becomes 29th state.

1848   Wisconsin becomes 30th state.

1849   Gold discovered at Sutter's Mill, CA.

1850   Compromise of 1850; President Zachary Taylor attends ceremonies
        at unfinished Washington Monument, July 4; becomes ill and dies, July 8;
        Millard Fillmore becomes 13th U.S. President; California becomes 31st state.

1852   Franklin Pierce becomes 14th U.S. President; *Uncle Tom's Cabin* published.

1854   Senator Stephen A. Douglas introduces bill to organize Nebraska Territory;
        Missouri Compromise repealed; Kansas-Nebraska Act passed;
        Republican party formed, Ripon, WI.

1857   Missouri Compromise declared unconstitutional; Dred Scott case.

1858   Minnesota becomes 32nd state; Lincoln-Douglas debates.

1859   Oregon becomes 33rd state; John Brown leads raid on Harpers Ferry, October 16;
        Brown is hanged, December 2.

1860   Lincoln elected, November 6; South Carolina secedes, December 20.

1861   Crittenden Compromise fails; six more states secede: Mississippi, Jan. 9;
        Florida, Jan. 10; Alabama, Jan. 11; Georgia, Jan 19; Louisiana, Jan. 26;
        Texas, February 1; Kansas becomes 34th state; Confederate forces fire
        on Fort Sumter, Charleston, SC; Civil War begins; Jefferson Davis becomes
        president of Confederacy, February 18; Lincoln inaugurated, March 4;
        calls for blockade of Southern ports, March 15.

Facts About Key Personalities

Cited below are some of the key figures in the Civil War during the period covered by this book. Listed are their main contributions and/or their main theaters of operation.

Anderson, Robert (1805-71): Kentucky-born army officer, West Point (1825); in command of Fort Sumter at time of Confederate attack, April 12, 1861.

Beauregard, Pierre Gustave Toutant (1818-93): Born New Orleans; West Point (1838); Confederate general in command of bombardment of Fort Sumter (1861); fought at Bull Run and Shiloh; commissioner of public works, New Orleans (1888).

Bell, John (1797-1869): Born Nashville, Tennessee; member U.S. House of Representatives (1827-41); U.S. Senate (1847-59); presidential nominee of Constitutional Union party (1860); carried only Tennessee, Kentucky, and Virginia.

Breckinridge, John Cabell (1821-75): Kentucky-born member of the U.S. House of Representatives (1851-55); U.S. vice president (1857-61); U.S. senator (1861); joined Confederate army (1861); secretary of war, Confederacy (1865).

Brown, John (1800-59): Born Torrington, Connecticut; abolitionist fanatic; known as Old Brown of Osawatomie for stand against raid by proslavery settlers (1856); seized arsenal at Harpers Ferry, Virginia (Oct. 16-17, 1859); convicted of treason against state of Virginia, hanged (Dec. 2); regarded as martyr by Northern sympathizers; remembered in marching song "John Brown's Body."

Buchanan, James (1791-1868): 15th president of the United States; born Mercersburg, Pennsylvania; served in War of 1812; House of Representatives (1821-31); minister to Russia (1832-34); U.S. senator (1834-45); secretary of state (1845-49); minister to Great Britain (1853-56); U.S. president (1857-61).

Clay, Henry (1777-1852): Self-educated Virginia-born lawyer; member of the House of Representatives (1811-14; 1815-21; 1823-25), U.S. Senate (1831-42), U.S. secretary of state (1825-29); nicknamed "Great Pacificator" for his work on Missouri Compromise (1820); reached height of statesmanship for his attempt to avoid civil war with the Compromise of 1850.

Crittenden, John Jordan (1786-1863): Kentucky-born senator (1817-19; 1835-41; 1842-48); Kentucky governor (1848-50); introduced Crittenden Compromise (defeated 1860) to ease tension between North and South.

Davis, Jefferson (1808-89): president, Confederate States of America; born Kentucky; West Point (1828); U.S. House of Representatives (1845-46); U.S. Senate (1847-51; 57-61); U.S. secretary of war (1853-57); captured in Georgia (May 10, 1865); imprisoned, indicted for treason, released (1867); retired to estate near Biloxi, Mississippi.

Doubleday, Abner (1819-1893): Born Ballston Spa, New York; West Point (1842); fired first return shot for the United States at Fort Sumter, 1861; served through Civil War and retired in 1873. Sometimes given credit for inventing the game of baseball.

Douglas, Stephen A. (1813-61): Born Brandon, Vermont; U.S. House of Representatives (1843-47); U.S. senator (1847-61); drafted Kansas-Nebraska bill (1854); engaged in prominent debates with Lincoln for Senate campaign of 1858.

Douglass, Frederick (1817?-95): Born Frederick Augustus Washington Bailey in Maryland, son of a slave woman and a white man; escaped in 1838 to Massachusetts where he changed his name and began to fight for blacks' freedom from slavery. Tireless and dedicated, his advice to any young black was "agitate!" Douglass was not above using outrage to get his point across. At an antislavery meeting in 1842, he said, "I appear this evening as a thief and a robber. I stole this head, these limbs, this body from my master, and ran off with them."

Fremont, John Charles (1813-90): Explorer, army officer; explored Oregon Territory, mapped Oregon Trail, reached California (1845); nominated for president by new Republican party (1856); defeated by Buchanan.

Geary, John W. (1819-73): territorial governor of Kansas during strife over slavery; resigned 1857; general in Civil War; governor of Pennsylvania (1867-73).

Hammond, James Henry (1807-64): Member of the House of Representatives (1835-36); governor of South Carolina (1842-44); U.S. senator (1857-60); advocate of states' rights; taunted Northern sympathizers (1858) with: "You dare not make war on cotton—no power on earth dares make war upon it. Cotton is king."

Pickens, Francis Wilkinson (1805-69): grandson of Revolutionary commander, Andrew Pickens; member of the House of Representatives (1834-43); minister to Russia (1858-60); governor of South Carolina when Sumter was attacked and Civil War began (1860-62).

Reeder, Andrew Horatio (1807-64): first governor of Kansas Territory (1854-55), appointed by President Pierce.

Robinson, Charles (1818-94): Massachusetts-born first governor of the state of Kansas (1861-63).

Scott, Dred (1795?-1858): Virginia-born slave and central figure in unsuccessful suit to win freedom on grounds of residence in free territory (decision 1857; see also Taney).

Stephens, Alexander Hamilton (1812-83): Georgia-born member of the House of Representatives (1843-59); vice president of the Confederacy (1861-65); returned to House (1873-82); governor of Georgia (1883).

Stowe, Harriet Beecher (1811-96): Born Connecticut; published *Uncle Tom's Cabin* (1852), which became a rallying symbol for abolitionists; collected works published (1896); elected to American Hall of Fame (1910).

Taney, Roger Brooke (1777-1864): American jurist; born in Maryland; succeeded John Marshall as Chief Justice, U.S. Supreme Court (1836); wrote the majority opinion of the Court in the Dred Scott case (1857).

Taylor, Zachary (1784-1850): 12th president of the United States (1849-50). Born in Virginia, fought in Mexican War; defeated Santa Anna at Buena Vista (1847); nicknamed "Old Rough and Ready."

Turner, Nat (1800-31): Virginia-born slave leader; plotted uprising (1831); captured and hanged (Nov. 11).

Wilmot, David (1814-68): Member House of Representatives (1845-51); introduced proviso prohibiting slavery in territory acquired in Mexican war.

Glossary

abolitionist	One who is against slavery.
arsenal	Collection of or storage place of weapons.
auction	Sale of property to the highest bidder.
blockade	Obstruction or isolation of generally an enemy area, such as a harbor, to prevent movement of persons or supplies.
bombardment	Heavy attack of artillery or aircraft.
candidate	A person running for office.
compromise	Settlement of differences reached by mutual concessions.
deadlock	State of inaction, a standstill.
Deep South	Usually includes U.S. states bordering the Gulf of Mexico.
fanatic	One with excessive enthusiasm for a cause, such as politics, or sport, such as a football team.
fugitive	One who flees, usually from arrest or peresectuion.
indentured servant	Person bound to work for another for a specified time.
militia	Part of a nation's organized armed forces liable to call only in an emergency.
pacificator	One who resolves conflicts without the use of force.
plantation	Agricultural estate usually worked by resident labor.
rebel	Disobedient person; one who takes arms against existing authority.
secession	Formal withdrawal from an organization.
slave trade	Buying and selling of blacks for profit prior to the Civil War.
stalemate	Same as deadlock.
states' rights	Those rights not given to the federal government by the U.S. Constitution nor forbidden by it to a separate state.
tariffs	Rates or charges imposed by government on imported goods.

Bibliography

American Heritage Book of the Presidents, 12 vols. New York: Dell, 1967.

Bradford, Ned. *Battles and Leaders of the Civil War.* New York: Appleton, 1956.

Catton, Bruce. *The American Heritage New History of the Civil War.* New York: Viking, 1996.

Commager, Henry Steele. *The Blue and the Gray.* New York: Bobbs-Merrill, 1950.

_____. *Documents of American History* Vol. 1. Upper Saddle River, NJ: Prentice Hall, 1988.

Davis, William C., ed. *The Civil War.* Alexandria, VA: Time-Life Books, 1983, 28 vols.

Gruver, Rebecca Brooks. *An American History*, Vol. 1. London: Addison-Wesley, 1972.

McPherson, James W. *For Cause & Comrades: Why Men Fought in the Civil War.* New York: Oxford Univ. Press, 1997.

Ward, Geoffrey C. *The Civil War: An Illustrated History.* New York: Knopf, 1990.

Further Reading

Allen, Robert. *Daniel Webster: Defender of the Union.* Milford, MI: Mott Media, 1980.

Bak, Richard. *The Day Lincoln Was Shot.* Dallas, TX: Taylor Publishing, 1998.

Coil, Suzanne M. *Harriet Beecher Stowe (Impact Biographies series).* Danbury, CT: Franklin Watts, 1993.

Cox, Clinton. *Fiery Vision: The Life and Death of John Brown.* New York: Scholastic, 1997.

Freedman, Suzanne. *Roger Taney: The Dred Scott Legacy (Justices of the Supreme Court series).* Springfield, NJ: Enslow, 1995.

Lester, Julius. *From Slave Ship to Freedom Road.* New York: Dial Books for Young Readers, 1998.

Potter, Robert R. *Jefferson Davis (American Troublemakers series).* Austin, TX: Raintree Steck-Vaughn, 1992.

Rutberg, Becky. *Mary Lincoln's Dressmaker.* New York: Walker, 1995.

Taylor, Kimberly Hayes. *Black Abolitionists and Freedom Fighters.* Minneapolis: Oliver Press, 1996.

Thomas, Hugh. *The Slave Trade: The Story of the Atlantic Slave Trade, 1440-1870.* New York: Simon & Schuster, 1997.

Thomas, Velma Maia. *Lest We Forget: The Passage from Africa to Slavery and Emancipation.* New York: Crown, 1997.

Websites

Here are a few suggested websites with information relevant to the contents of this book. The authors and the editors take no responsibility for the accuracy of any information found on the Internet. Nor can we guarantee the availability of any website.

Abraham Lincoln Online
Everything about Honest Abe, from speeches to photographs and a Quiz of the Month. You can even join an online discussion.
http://www.netins.net/showcase/creative/lincoln. html

Causes of the Civil War: The Compromise of 1820 and the Early Anti-slavery Movement (article)
A monthly article on various Civil War topics as well as reviews of the best Civil War websites.
http://www.suite101.com/articles/article.cfm/3848

Christine's Genealogy Website
African American genealogy Website featuring Freedmen's Bureau records, lists of emigrants to Liberia, census records, manumission records, fugitive slave cases and links. *http://ccharity.com/*

Fort Sumter
Throughout March of 1861, the Confederate authorities sought to drive out the Union occupants of Fort Sumter peacefully. However, when Abraham Lincoln's administration refused to surrender the fort, things took on more violent action.
http://tqd.advanced.org/3055/graphics/experience/battles/fortsumter.html

The Fugitive Slave Act
The Fugitive Slave Act is part of the painful legacy of slavery in the United States. Essentially, it mandated the return of runaway slaves, regardless of where in the Union they were found. *http://www.csusm.edu/public/guests/history/docs/fsact.html*

Harriet Tubman Historical Society
Encourages and supports research, plays, and programs and educates the world about the legacy of Harriet Tubman and all patriots for freedom. *http://www.harriettubman.com/*

Origins of the Underground Railroad
Information on the organization and operations of the Underground Railroad
http://www.niica.on.ca/csonan/UNDERGROUND.htm

Index

Note: Page numbers in italics indicate illustrations or maps.

Index

Index

Index

Acknowledgments

Cover & Title Page, Corbis-Bettmann; p.7, The Granger Collection, New York; p.10, Library of Congress LC-USZ262-114376; p.14, Corbis-Bettmann; p.19, The Granger Collection, New York; p. 23 (l), The Granger Collection, New York; p. 23 (r), Library of Congress LC-USZ62-10476; p. 25 Corbis-Bettmann; p. 26 Library of Congress; p. 29, Abby Aldrich Rockefeller Folk Art Center, Williamsburg, VA; p. 31, Corbis-Bettmann; p. 36, Brown Brothers; p. 37, National Portrait Gallery, The Smithsonian Institution; p. 38, The Granger Collection, New York; p. 40 Courtesy Boston Public Library; p. 43, The Kansas State Historical Society; p. 44, Kansas State Historical Society; p. 46 North Wind Pictures; p. 47, Corbis-Bettmann; p. 50, Library of Congress LC-USZ62-64979; p. 53, Library of Congress LC-D43-T01-1756; p. 54, Library of Congress LC-USZ62-121733; p. 57, Corbis-Bettmann; p. 59, Corbis-Bettmann; p. 62, Library of Congress, LC-USZ62-5884; p. 66, The Granger Collection, New York; p. 69 Library of Congress, LC-USZC4-4583; p. 71, The National Archives/Corbis; p. 75, Corbis-Bettmann; p. 80, CORBIS; p. 82, CORBIS; p. 83, Collection of the New York Historical Society; p. 86, National Archives NWDNS-111-B-4183; p. 88, Library of Congress, LC-USZC2-1990; p. 91, CORBIS; p. 93, National Archives NWDNS-121-BA-914A; p. 95, CORBIS; p. 96 (l), Indianapolis Museum of Art, James E. Roberts Fund; p. 96 (r), Cook Collection, Valentine Museum, Richmond, VA; p. 98, Rhode Island Historical Association.

Map design & production: Tina Graziano, MapQuest.com